He Was Here

He Was Here

Those Who Knew Jesus Speak

Ivan J. Kauffman

Brazos Press
A Division of Baker Book House Co
Grand Rapids, Michigan 49516

© 2000 by Ivan J. Kauffman

Published by Brazos Press
a division of Baker Book House Company
P.O. Box 6287, Grand Rapids, MI 49516-6287

Printed in the United States of America

Library of Congress Cataloging-in-Publication Data

Kauffman, Ivan J., 1938–
    He was here : those who knew Jesus speak / Ivan J. Kauffman.
        p.   cm.
    ISBN 1-58743-005-3 (cloth)
    1. Jesus Christ—Poetry. 2. Bible. N.T.—History of Biblical
events—Poetry. I. Title.

PS3561.A818 H4 2001
844'.54—dc21   00-050767

For current information about all releases from Brazos Press, visit our web site:
http://www.brazospress.com

Dedication

For Lois
Who knows why

Contents

Preface

We have ended one time and begun another. Never before in human history have we counted time from the same event for two thousand years, until now.

On the one hand it means nothing. All the ways we mark time are arbitrary. There have been many calendars in the past, there are many now, there will be many others in the future. But still we have chosen this particular event as the base for our calendar, and as we begin a third millennium from it we can hardly avoid looking back, to the event that took place when our time began.

We each have opinions about that time, the event that took place, and what it means. We have only this in common, that we each have an opinion. For the life that stands at the beginning of our calendar has so impacted human history it cannot be ignored.

Just as the events of 1999 were connected to those of 1998, and those of the year 2000 were connected to those of 1999, so every year's events have been connected to those of the previous year, in an unbroken line stretching back to the year 1. That is not actually the year Jesus was born—he was probably a child of about five then, we're not sure—but there is a reason we count time in close approximation from this birth, for everything that has happened since has been marked by it.

One need not be a believer to acknowledge this. Even if one finds Jesus' impact on human history insignificant, or even harmful, there can be little argument that his life has had a major impact on our civilization, and that it continues to affect millions of people at a very deep level.

When we began the third Christian millennium we also ended what was almost certainly the most eventful century in human history. Between the years 1900 and 2000 human life throughout the world was transformed to a degree we find difficult to comprehend. Everything around us has changed—the way we think and speak, the way we are governed, the way we communicate, the way we travel, even the way our families are formed.

But we have not changed. Our emotions and our passions, our need for food, for shelter, for love, for acceptance are no different than they were a thousand years ago—or two thousand years ago, or twenty thousand years ago.

The twentieth century tended to forget these very human facts. This was instead a century of theories, each promising a better life for everyone if only its ideas and concepts were adopted. Virtually every conceivable theory was proposed at some point during the century, and many were actually put into practice. People by the millions gave their lives for these theories—some willingly, most unwillingly.

In the end we lost confidence in the theories, all of them. They seemed always to omit something necessary for human life, and we were left with a terrible emptiness, a hunger we could not fill.

And so we have returned to the stories, where we find a kind of truth the theories lack. People like my children, who grew up after the cultural revolution of the 1960s, often communicate by referring to scenes from the stories told in movies and television. They have become an essential part of our common language.

The most popular story, the one most often told, is the one that took place when our calendar began. But we most often know this story only in fragments—bits and pieces heard in the churches when we were listening. Occasionally we also hear it told in our literature and entertainment, but often inaccurately. Each year at Christmas and Easter this great story comes into our lives, running through our culture like a river, but it is a river we seldom drink from, or swim in, or launch our boats on.

But when we lose touch with this story—whether we are religious or not—something vital leaves our lives. For our culture to a large extent formed around it, and when we no longer take the time to learn its lessons and absorb its wisdom we become spiritually exhausted and culturally discontented.

The new epoch that began with the great international cultural revolution of the 1960s has been called postmodern. That name is accurate, so far as it goes, for a turn away from theory, and from the certainty theory promises, has indeed replaced the old era's confidence in human rationality.

The era we call modern lasted for nearly five hundred years. It rested on two basic assumptions: that only what is visible and measurable is real, and that only what is obviously logical to humans can be true. Science, which limited itself to the visible and the measurable, and which rejected all it could not understand, became this era's *de facto* religion. The many theories proposed in the twentieth century all claimed a basis in science.

Christian theology made a determined effort to adapt its beliefs to the modern era's assumptions, but in the end only succeeded in making itself vaguely ridiculous. Christian faith has always been based on very different assumptions—the beliefs that the real is more than the visible, and that human experience includes much that cannot be understood by the logical mind.

Some theorists, both Christian and otherwise, believe the collapse of the old theories will be followed by some new theory that is free from the defects that destroyed the old. But to believe this is to attempt to continue a discredited past into a future inhabited by persons seeking something entirely new to live by. The postmodern era—whatever it will eventually be called— belongs to those who approach reality as infinite, and who are humble enough to realize that reality will always transcend our understanding of it.

To enter this new era we must learn a new language, for the language of theory and the language of life are fundamentally different—as different as the language in this essay is from the language in the stories it introduces. We of course need both: language for the left brain and language for the right, language that analyzes and language that combines. In the era now ended, language that analyzed, that took apart and distinguished, was dominant. In the era we are beginning, the language of relationship will have equal standing.

That is why poetry will be restored to its natural place in the new era. For poetry is the language of relationship, the voice of love, the word not limited to a single meaning, used in all its power. In order for reality to be understood in all its complexity, poetry must take its rightful place alongside philosophy and science, for certain portions of reality can only be perceived poetically.

———

There are two poetic traditions existing side by side in Western civilization. The best known one has its origins in ancient Greek culture. Its earliest surviving works are the poems of Homer, probably written in the eighth century before Christ. This tradition equates poetry with verbal technique—especially ornamentation, regular meter, rhyme, and frequent similes and allusions. It is predominantly mythical in orientation. When we are taught poetry in the schools, those poets who have written in this tradition are the ones we study.

The second tradition has its origins in the ancient Semitic cultures, and is known to us from the Hebrew literature preserved in the Bible. Its earliest works are from Moses' time, in the thirteenth century before Christ, but the best known and most influential poems were composed by King David of Jerusalem, who founded that city in the tenth century before Christ. A later Hebrew literary master gave us the great poems in Second Isaiah and Job in the sixth century before Christ.

The Biblical tradition equates poetry with a message. Technique is present here, but it is always secondary to content, serving the message, making sure it is conveyed. There is no art for

11

art's sake here. Here the word always points beyond itself, to its meaning. And here the words chosen come from ordinary speech, for this tradition rejects all elitism. There is rhythm and rhyme but they serve the thought; there is verbal beauty and allusion but they exist only to make the message more clear.

The message this tradition embodies is that there is only a single God, who created and continues to order all reality, both what is known to humans and what is not. This single, active God is present in history, sometimes acting in ways very different from the ordinary—what we call miracles—but most often acting in predictable ways, giving life to individual persons, establishing justice in human affairs.

The believing artist adopts both these traditions. The artist's job is to describe human reality as it actually exists. Whatever is there must be placed on the canvas, the page, the stage. We are not allowed to judge anything, to ignore anything, to change anything. If we do not comply with these stern rules what results is propaganda, not art.

The believer's task is similar, but different. To believe is to see the universe and all the persons and things in it not only as they appear to us but also as they appear when viewed from their source. To believe is to see human life in context—to look beyond the obvious, beyond what even can be imagined—to see ourselves as we are seen by the divine force who created us.

Jesus himself displays this ability to a supreme degree in the parables, simultaneously telling the truth about what is in the world and what could be, about what everyone sees and what only he could see. The result combines great art and profound truth, both completely accessible to everyone—persons of all conditions and all ages, in all cultures and all times. His example defines what it means to be a Christian artist.

Above all, both the artist's job and the believer's job is to tell the truth, and to the extent that we are actually able to tell the truth we have succeeded both as artists and as Christians. Dante did this, and all who follow him walk in the path he pioneered. Blake too followed this road, and took it into the English language. Without these two exceptionally courageous lives this book could not have been written. Indeed the boundary between the sacred and the secular is very thin for all artists. This includes Shakespeare, whose work has given us language to express our deepest and truest thoughts, and the courage to display them in public.

To be truthful is to be naked, for when the truth is told nothing can be hidden. Our weaknesses are revealed, our selfishness seen—along with our goodness, and the divine spark within us all. Here morality, the behavior we expect from ourselves and from others, and which we try so hard to achieve, takes second place to honesty, for here the good and the true are one. Those who clothe themselves in garments designed to conceal, those who wish to appear other than they really are, can enter either the world of art or the world of belief, but not both. The truth as beauty can only be seen in the spaces where we actually live.

That is why there can never be a separate language for belief— words different than the ones we use when we buy groceries, or tell a joke, or argue with our husbands. When that split between the religious and the ordinary occurs, as it so often does, belief inevitably becomes detached from our real lives, moving into a mythical space where a special religious language has an arbitrary relevance, but where no one actually lives.

Jesus and Paul in the first century went to the places where people actually lived and spoke to them in their ordinary language, using images and idioms everyone understood. All too often in subsequent times—and especially in the century just ended—the Church has instead asked people to come to it, insisting when they did that they learn a new language used only in the churches. The result has been to reduce belief to a hobby, practiced only by a few who derive pleasure from it, while the great masses wait outside.

In the medieval period the Biblical stories were often presented as popular dramas, frequently out of doors on the steps to the churches. Some of these early dramas are still performed in European villages, and are remembered as the medieval mystery plays. They are studied by literary historians for their role in founding the European dramatic tradition, and are occasionally still performed in academic settings. As a student at the Earlham School of Religion in 1966 I directed one of the medieval Biblical dramas for the Earlham College May Day celebration.

Several English authors continued this centuries-old tradition in the twentieth century, most notably Dorothy L. Sayers. In the 1930s she had achieved best-seller status as the author of the Lord Peter Whimsey detective novels, but with the coming of World War II she turned her considerable talents to religious topics. Her most popular work in this period was *The Man Born to Be King*, a series of radio plays on the life of Jesus, broadcast in 1942 to very large audiences by the BBC. It was later published as a book and became a best seller.

In the introduction Ms. Sayers says, "Not Herod, not Caiphus, not Pilate, not Judas ever contrived to fasten upon Jesus Christ the reproach of insipidity; that final indignity was left for pious hands to inflict." She adds, "You have forgotten, perhaps, that it is, first and foremost, a story—a true story, the turning point of history, 'the only thing that has ever really happened.'"

After completing *The Man Born to Be King* Ms. Sayers devoted the remainder of her life to translating Dante's *Divine Comedy* into English.

T. S. Eliot, the American poet who returned to England and to the religion his ancestors had abandoned, also in his later years turned his formidable talents to writing drama for the churches. His poem *The Journey of the Magi* had a major role in inspiring this work.

But the idiom and the language in this book are American rather than English. The author was born and educated in the very center of the North American continent, in the states of Colorado and Kansas, and the dialect and the culture of this difficult land—where the prairie and the desert meet, and the

American dream ended in the blinding dust storms and the terrible depression of the 1930s—are his mother tongue and his native culture. What we know most truly and deeply we know in our native tongue.

Many other American writers have translated the Gospels into our language, especially for the stage, and their works are frequently performed in our churches. In the 1960s the musical *Godspell* brought the Gospels to the American commercial stage with great success. In the 1980s an American priest, Fr. Joseph Girzone, retold the Gospel story in a popular novel, *Joshua*, set in our times.

All these are efforts to connect our still emerging American culture to our much older spiritual roots. We brought these roots with us from Europe—along with the theology, the rituals, the hymns, the architecture, and the institutions that sustained them. But America is not Europe and we are still engaged in creating a new tradition, connected to our past, but also true to our experience here.

In America we have no kings, and only a very short past. When we doubt, we have only a new and still unformed tradition to turn to. When we fear for our survival, we have only a short history to reassure us. And so we turn to what works in the present, ever ready to abandon it if it does not work. For us the only authority is experience.

Religion is both what most sustains us and also what most divides us. Time for us exists primarily in the future, and without the hope that faith provides we could not go on. But in the end faith for us is a private matter, and we have produced an almost infinite number of creeds and beliefs, each of which must be taken with equal seriousness.

We are profoundly democratic, not only in the way our government is conducted, but even more in the way we perceive reality. We do not believe any authority, any expert, comprehends the whole truth. And we believe every person, however lowly or lim-

15

ited, has something to add to the store of human knowledge and human wisdom.

That is why the human Jesus is so important to us, for we sense in his life an openness to all people—strong and weak, poor and rich, saint and sinner, established and outcast. The identity of Christian faith with an aristocracy, or a privileged elite, is entirely foreign to us. For us the churches have been the means by which those on the margins have found their way into the mainstream.

What constitutes authority here is the capacity to make the ordinary lives of ordinary people better in some way. We have found the stories about Jesus from the Gospels do that, and again and again, week after week, year after year, we tell them in our churches.

We have found the theology produced by the philosophers less helpful. It seems always to produce more arguments than solutions. We know what it is to be lost and to be found, but not what it is to understand. That is why "Amazing Grace" is our favorite hymn, sung in all the churches despite our differing theologies. Living as we do on the raw edge, we seldom have the luxury to ignore our defects, and so for us radical deep-level change—what we call conversion—is central to our religion. We do not believe you can be good simply by trying. We have tried and found it is impossible.

We have also learned in this often brutal land that the stories about Jesus are true. We have those who argue otherwise, but they have not been able to help us live. Why, we ask, if the stories are not true, have they been able to grip us generation after generation, in every time and place—whether we are child or elder, wealthy or poor, privileged or pariah? What else but the truth could have this power? What except the real could endure, and grow in popularity century after century?

The characters who speak in these thirty-three stories come to us from the first-century Mediterranean world, but they have joined us in our postmodern world—sharing our troubles, our dreams, our lives.

What they have in common is at some point having encountered Jesus face to face. Some knew him well, others only slightly. Some knew him as a friend, others as a problem. Some understood him, others completely missed the point. Some decided to follow him, others helped destroy him. They are like us.

These people encountered Jesus first in the inn, where strangers are entertained. It is here that Jesus enters human history. Next they met him in their homes, where ordinary life occurs. It is here that Jesus' healing power becomes evident.

They then met him in their temples, where we gather to recognize a divine reality that transcends the visible. It was here that Jesus left his most visible mark on human history. And finally they encountered Jesus in their palaces, the place where human society is governed and given structure. It was here that Jesus would be executed.

Wherever they met him, whatever their past or their present condition, people were changed by this encounter—even those who rejected him. The whole human family is here, in these stories, and we are all accepted by him, not as we should be but as we could be.

There is no greater privilege, no experience more life-giving, than leaving our places as spectators outside these stories and moving inside them—allowing them to be transformed from myth into actual event, taking place in our own lives and in our own time and place. It is a form of prayer.

HOLY THURSDAY
1999

.

The Former Theologian

The former theologian resembles the
thin, slightly ascetic philosopher in
the Rembrandt portrait, except that he
wears workman's clothing and has hands
obviously used to manual labor. His voice is
intelligent, but conveys commitment rather
than argument. In his manner he suggests
both gravity and freedom. His role, he has
come to understand, is to make the stories
available to others, so they can decide for
themselves what they mean.

THE FORMER THEOLOGIAN

I used to explain
Until I came to understand
We do not understand.

So I quit my job at the seminary and joined the circus.

I was ill prepared.
Entering the ring with the animals and trapeze artists,
Letting those judge who had paid admissions.

The tricks we tried at first did not succeed.
So I began telling stories
About those who knew him when he was here.

You may find them familiar.

They laugh, they lie.
They have sex, they wash the dishes.
They burp, they pay the bills.

Some believe, some argue.
Some are healed, some judge.
Some eat with him, some only watch.
They are like us. None is qualified to preach.

They tell you their stories to make you happy.

    If they succeed
    You must decide.

part one

THE INN

In the inn we confront Jesus as a stranger—someone we weren't expecting and don't quite know what to do with. But despite our discomfort and confusion he is here, and somehow we must make room for him.

The
Innkeeper

The innkeeper is a Mediterranean Archie
Bunker. He is well fed and has a large
paunch, which is covered by a bartender's
apron tied around the front. He is smoking
a large cigar, which he waves about as he
speaks. He is in firm command of his small
establishment. He is also a man in a
hurry—in constant motion, although he
appears to have no place to go. This is a
person completely focused on the here-
and-now and what's-in-it-for-me?
His voice is bellowing and forceful.

The Biblical Account
of the Birth of Jesus

In those days a decree went out from Caesar Augustus that the whole world should be enrolled. This was the first enrollment, when Quirinius was governor of Syria. So all went to be enrolled, each to his own town.

And Joseph too went up from Galilee from the town of Nazareth to Judea, to the city of David that is called Bethlehem, because he was of the house and family of David, to be enrolled with Mary, his betrothed, who was with child.

While they were there, the time came for her to have her child, and she gave birth to her firstborn son. She wrapped him in swaddling clothes and laid him in a manger, because there was no room for them in the inn.

THE INNKEEPER

Hey, gimme a break.
I'm tired a takin' crap,
All this no-room-in-the-inn bull.

Lemme tell you somethin'
All you big Mr. I-Woulda-Let-'Em-Ins,
You can't get excited every time a woman has a baby.
Women get pregnant all the time,
Somebody's gotta do the work.

Sure, if I'd a know'd who it was I'd a made room.
Lord I'd be a millionaire.
Put up a sign says, "Jesus Christ Was Born Here,"
They'd line up all the way out to the Dead Sea tryin' to get in.
I ain't stupid.

But let me tell you about this place.
We're talkin' a bunch a camel drivers,
And some gypsy women turnin' tricks.
You know what I mean.
We wasn't exactly expectin' any Big Religious Events.

And anyway, they looked like a couple a kids to me.
She had pimples and he was scared to death.
Not the kind had any money to spend.
And I'll be honest with you,
I make my livin' sellin' booze by the drink and beds by the hour.
I ain't in this for my health.

The only way you know about me is they wouldn't go away.
Even when I sicced the dogs on 'em they just stood there.

There was somethin' about her face.
Her eyes was blue, but she was awful dark.
Almost black, you know what I mean.
Course it was pitch dark out there, you couldn't see a thing.

Anyway she had her baby out in the stable.
My wife went out and helped her some.
Some a the sheepherders thought it was a big deal.
Me, I stayed inside'n took care a the payin' guests.

  Sure, I believe it now. Who doesn't?
  But let's tell it like it is.
  If they came again I'd do the same thing.

        How you supposed to know?
        It's all so ordinary.

        You can't get excited
        Every time a woman has a baby.

The
Innkeeper's Wife

The innkeeper's wife is an earth mother,
as strong as her husband but in a very
different way. They are partners,
completely dependent on each other, but
she is much more aware of this than he.
As she speaks she wipes her hands on
her apron and cleans the table, which her
husband has left covered with crumbs.
She is both competent and resigned, and
her voice conveys this. Like her husband,
she is obviously well fed.

THE INNKEEPER'S WIFE

Women help women.
That's how we're different than men.

We gotta be.
What does a man know about bringin' life into this world?

To hear 'em talk you'd think they'd never been born.
Most of 'em can't even stand to watch.

And then they talk about how tough they are.

Well, let me tell you something, it ain't easy havin' a baby
And until you've done it it's all talk.

  It's bad enough at home,
  With your mother there.

  If you have one.
  Most of us die before our kids grow up.

She was just a girl.
And out there in the stable . . .

You act like it was all so pretty,
Puttin' up those things at Christmas
With everybody just come from the beauty shop.
Well let me tell you Mrs. Martha Clean-and-Nice
These people hadn't been to no beauty shop. Ever.

And let me tell you about this stable. It stinks.
Rats crawlin' around under the hay.

There weren't no pretty little lights.
And I didn't see no halos.

When mornin' came there was blood on the ground.
And sweat runnin' down her face.
Even when she was shiverin' from the cold.

It wasn't no different than any other birth.
She had a big smile when she saw the baby.

They're all miracles. Even the men know that.
You can tell by the looks on their face.

But Lord, what pain they cost us.
And what a bloody mess afterwards.

    It seems like you can't do anything in this world
    Without hurtin' somebody,
    And a big mess to clean up afterwards.

    And it's always the women who have to do it.

The
Sheepherder

The sheepherder is dressed in a sheepskin
garment and carries a shepherd's staff. His
dog is with him. He lives outdoors and
comes inside only occasionally, bringing
with him nature's wisdom. His speech is as
economical as possible, the silences often
more important than the words. His voice is
soft but not weak. He is naturally reserved,
but is now deeply excited. As he speaks he
constantly glances through the doorway,
looking up at the sky.

Now there were shepherds in that region living in the fields and keeping the night watch over their flock. The angel of the Lord appeared to them and the glory of the Lord shone around them, and they were struck with great fear.

The angel said to them, "Do not be afraid; for behold, I proclaim to you good news of great joy that will be for all the people. For today in the city of David a savior has been born for you who is Messiah and Lord. And this will be a sign for you: you will find an infant wrapped in swaddling clothes and lying in a manger."

And suddenly there was a multitude of the heavenly host with the angel, praising God and saying:

> *"Glory to God in the highest*
> *and on earth peace to those on whom his favor rests."*

When the angels went away from them to heaven, the shepherds said to one another, "Let us go, then, to Bethlehem to see this thing that has taken place, which the Lord has made known to us."

So they went in haste and found Mary and Joseph, and the infant lying in the manger. When they saw this, they made known the message that had been told them about this child.

All who heard it were amazed by what had been told them by the shepherds.

LUKE 2:8–18

THE SHEEPHERDER

Saw 'em first
Climbin' the hill
Outside a town.

Could tell they come a long way.
Walkin' real sore. Holdin' her belly.
Him tryin' to help.

Dark comin' on.
There weren't no place for 'em in town.

Would a ask 'em to stay with us.
But don't have no place ourselves.

Could tell it was time.
Watchin' sheep just about always know
When a lamb's comin'.

Can't rightly say
Everything happened that night.

One thing sure, nobody ever heard singin' like that.
Went right to a man's soul.
Truth was, thought we was goners.
Would a run off,
But the sheep was there.

And the ones singin'.
Calmed us down
Got us thinkin' straight.

Men started sayin', "Gotta listen to this."
Others said, "Can't leave the sheep."

But we did.
Went runnin' into town like it was payday.
Woke up some people gettin' there.

Found the baby.
Like the music said.

Couldn't figure out why more didn't come.
Must a not seen what we did.

Folks miss a lot sleepin' inside.

Tried to tell people.
Most wanted to keep sleepin'.
Rest told us we was nuts.

Couldn't happen.
Just a bunch a sheepherders.
What did we know?

    Said, want a know what's goin' on?
    Ask a expert.

Anna
the Prophet

The prophet is old and stooped over, her
face covered with wrinkles, like Mother
Teresa. Her eyes are bright and clear, like a
child's. She is beaming with excitement and
obviously has something important to tell
us. Her voice is quiet and peaceful, but also
convinced and powerful. As she speaks she
constantly looks up, searching for the next
word, which produces gaps in her speech,
as age has produced gaps in her teeth.
The boundary between the present and
the eternal has long ago begun to dissolve
for her.

THE BIBLICAL ACCOUNT
OF JESUS' PRESENTATION IN THE TEMPLE

When the days were completed for their purification according to the law of Moses, they took him up to Jerusalem to present him to the Lord.

There was also a prophetess, Anna, the daughter of Phanuel, of the tribe of Asher. She was advanced in years, having lived seven years with her husband after her marriage, and then as a widow until she was eighty-four.

She never left the temple, but worshiped night and day with fasting and prayer.

And coming forward at that very time, she gave thanks to God and spoke about the child to all who were awaiting the redemption of Jerusalem.

LUKE 2:22, 36–38

ANNA THE PROPHET

He's here!
What we're waiting for.

His parents came to the temple this morning!
Cutest little thing!

Every baby, we always wondered, is this the one?
Then we'd say, "Maybe the next one."

The Romans told us to stop.
They said, "We're it. Get used to it."

But all they had was soldiers, what could they do?
Make work for the gravediggers.
If that's all there is, why bother?
We don't need more dead bodies to bury.

We need people to pray.
It's the only thing that works.

I'm eighty-four years old.
People ask me why I don't give up.
I say, "I'm waiting."
They say, "What for?"
I say, "The same thing you are."

That's why you can't get on a train if you don't have a ticket.
You wouldn't know when to get off.

People don't understand that.

They say, "What you see is what you get."
But what you see is what you're lookin' for.

Forget about the pie-in-the-sky-by-and-by stuff.
Dreams never turn out the way we think.

There's got to be real babies.
Somebody you can feel their heart beat.
Change their diapers.

People who pray understand.
The others mostly stand around and argue.

Who ever changed anything arguing?
The prayers, they're up to Yahweh,
Who knows what Yahweh can do?

That should make even the sourpusses happy.

Well, it's time for me to go now.
But you—you stay and have a party.

Sing a lot,
Kiss the girls,
Be happy.

It's gonna be a great time.

The
Wise Men

The wise men are at the end of a long
journey, which has brought them to a
strange land, a place they never expected
to be. They are both amazed and awed.
Their spokesman's voice is thoughtful and
grave—filled with an unconscious but
profound dignity. He speaks slowly and
deliberately, with every word considered.
The clothing they wear indicates they
belong to a very ancient tradition, and their
bearing makes it clear they intend to
continue the tradition they have inherited.

THE BIBLICAL ACCOUNT
OF THE VISIT OF THE MAGI

When Jesus was born in Bethlehem of Judea, in the days of King Herod, behold, magi from the east arrived in Jerusalem, saying, "Where is the newborn king of the Jews? We saw his star at its rising and have come to do him homage."

When King Herod heard this, he was greatly troubled, and all Jerusalem with him. Assembling all the chief priests and the scribes of the people, he inquired of them where the Messiah was to be born. They said to him, "In Bethlehem of Judea, for thus it has been written through the prophet."

Then Herod called the magi secretly and ascertained from them the time of the star's appearance. He sent them to Bethlehem and said, "Go and search diligently for the child. When you have found him, bring me word, that I too may go and do him homage."

After their audience with the king they set out. And behold, the star that they had seen at its rising preceded them, until it came and stopped over the place where the child was.

They were overjoyed at seeing the star, and on entering the house they saw the child with Mary his mother. They prostrated themselves and did him homage. Then they opened their treasures and offered him gifts of gold, frankincense, and myrrh.

And having been warned in a dream not to return to Herod, they departed for their country by another way.

MATTHEW 2:1–5, 7–12

THE WISE MEN

We came here looking for the king
Wisdom had promised us.

For many thousand years we had known
The universe has a plan,
That all real power is above us.

Now the time had come.
Saddle up the camels, take our treasures from the safe,
Embark on a journey whose end we did not know.

Our colleagues urged delay.
"Continue your studies," they said.
"Stay home until you are certain."

But how is it possible to know if you know
Unless you act?
Connect the mind and the body and see what happens?

There were the usual difficulties en route.
Snakes in the desert, thieves in the mountains,
Seduction in the oases.

But all these we had known before,
Having reached the age when such are
Merely irritants.

What made this journey so extraordinarily difficult
Were the politics.

We had departed expecting a great king
Able to reward us.
What we found was quite different.

A child, a mother, a father,
Each living for the other. No more.

And a king who feared their power.
It was astonishingly simple.

We left them our gifts,
Not knowing what use would be made of them.

Then, disobeying the king's orders,
We once again followed the inner voices,
Returning to our homeland by a different route.

Our colleagues, of course, will want to know:
What did we see?
What actions did we take?
What lessons were learned?

We will tell them,
Having come here on established roads,
We learned they lead always to death.

That if we wish to go on
We must find a way
That protects the child.

wife

What one notices at once about Herod's wife is her clothing, which unmistakably indicates she can wear anything she chooses, whatever the cost. But as she speaks our attention is drawn from her gaudy clothing to the pain etched on her face, leaving creases her heavy makeup and conspicuous jewelry cannot conceal. She continually looks down at her hands or over her shoulder, as if fearing something, and there is an immense weariness in her voice. She speaks as though she is alone in the world.

The Biblical Account
of the Massacre of the Innocents

When Herod realized that he had been deceived by the magi, he became furious.

He ordered the massacre of all the boys in Bethlehem and its vicinity two years old and under, in accordance with the time he had ascertained from the magi.

Then was fulfilled what had been said through Jeremiah the prophet:

"A voice was heard in Ramah,
        sobbing and loud lamentation;
Rachel weeping for her children,
        and she would not be consoled,
        since they were no more."

MATTHEW 2: 16–18

HEROD'S WIFE

It was awful. Just awful.
The worst thing we'd ever done.

I tried to be strong but it was just too much.
All those dead babies . . .

One woman had twins.
She came all the way up to the palace gates
Screaming so loud you could hear her in the dining room.

And we had visitors from Rome that day.

    We had to tell the soldiers to kill her too.
    And then her other children started screaming.

    It was awful. Just awful.
    The worst thing we ever did.

And all because some "wise men" showed up
From back east. Idiot intellectuals,
Always asking questions they don't have to answer.

This place was a dump when we got it,
Grass growing down the middle of the street,
Nobody had anything.

We built docks so the ships would come,
Fixed up the temple to make the priests happy,
Sent money to Rome whether we had it or not.

You think it's fun being king?
You should try it some time; it's mostly trouble.
You put out one fire, they start two more.

If people would help it wouldn't be so bad,
But everybody wants the king to do it.

I told my husband just ignore them.
"You've killed enough people," I said.
"We've only got a few years left.
Can't we have some peace and quiet before we die?"

But he said, "You can't take chances.
Anybody makes trouble, we're the ones who pay."

What could I say?
Everybody knows you can't have but one king at a time.

    But that day when the soldiers came home,
    Babies' blood all over their uniforms,
    I confess: I no longer wanted to be Queen.

    There has to be a better way.

Joseph
the Carpenter

Joseph is dressed as a carpenter and is seated at a table, which he could have made. There is an air of nobility about him, but without any sense of privilege in his bearing or attitude. This is a man who makes things happen without expecting any reward other than knowing he has caused something to happen that needed to happen. His voice is matter of fact, but conveys real surprise at the story he is telling. He runs his hand over the table as he speaks.

The Biblical Account
of Joseph the Husband of Mary

When his mother Mary was betrothed to Joseph, but before they lived together, she was found with child through the holy Spirit. Joseph her husband, since he was a righteous man, yet unwilling to expose her to shame, decided to divorce her quietly.

Such was his intention when, behold, the angel of the Lord appeared to him in a dream and said, "Joseph, son of David, do not be afraid to take Mary your wife into your home."

When Joseph awoke, he did as the angel of the Lord had commanded him and took his wife into his home.

When [the magi] had departed, behold, the angel of the Lord appeared to Joseph in a dream and said, "Rise, take the child and his mother, flee to Egypt, and stay there until I tell you. Herod is going to search for the child to destroy him."

Joseph rose and took the child and his mother by night and departed for Egypt.

MATTHEW 1:18–20, 24; 2:13–14

JOSEPH THE CARPENTER

Who can say what a son is?

Had I not cared for him you would never have known him,
But from the beginning I knew he was not mine,
That I would never establish a dynasty as my ancestor David did.

Not that I decided this.
My only part in his life was to act on my dreams.

My story is much like your own,
Difficult to square with morality, and often embarrassing.

    How is one to know what to do
    When Yahweh changes the rules?

At first I was nearly mad with shame.
Unwed pregnancies are punished by death here.

When Mary's condition became known
I dared not leave my house
For fear my neighbors would insult me.

Then the great dream came
And I had to choose between it and my shame.

    It was then I learned how much easier it is
    To be ashamed than to believe.

    There are rules for shame,
    But belief must always be done despite the rules.

Some there are who delight in breaking laws,
But I am not among them.
To me rules are like roads that lead to known places.

But instead I had to learn to follow my dreams,
For without dreams there are no roads.

My namesake, our father Israel's favorite,
He was also a dreamer.

His brothers sent him across the desert into Egypt
Where he told Pharaoh the meaning of his dreams.

We too traveled to Egypt.
That was the second dream.

We were safe there for a time,
And learned many strange and wonderful things.

But in the end we returned to our homeland.
It too is a dream become a place.

    And now when I hear you say
    "It was only a dream,"
    I wonder if you understand
    What would have happened
    Had I said the same.

Mary's
Mother

Mary's mother is one of us, a grandmother
dedicated to continuing the generations.
As she speaks she puts the house in order
so that life can go on. Others have been
using its space; she knows someone must
make it livable. She projects great dignity,
which comes from knowing her role in life
is essential. Her voice is strong but gentle.
Like her son-in-law Joseph she is
astonished at the story she tells, but also
like him she has come to understand
its meaning.

THE BIBLICAL ACCOUNT
OF THE PREGNANCY OF MARY

The angel Gabriel was sent from God to a town of Galilee called Nazareth, to a virgin betrothed to a man named Joseph, of the house of David, and the virgin's name was Mary.

And coming to her, he said, "Hail, favored one! The Lord is with you." But she was greatly troubled at what was said and pondered what sort of greeting this might be.

Then the angel said to her, "Do not be afraid, Mary, for you have found favor with God. Behold, you will conceive in your womb and bear a son, and you shall name him Jesus. He will be great and will be called Son of the Most High. . . ."

But Mary said to the angel, "How can this be, since I have no relations with a man?"

And the angel said to her in reply, "The holy Spirit will come upon you, and the power of the Most High will overshadow you. . . .

"And behold, Elizabeth, your relative has also conceived a son in her old age, and this is the sixth month for her who was called barren; for nothing will be impossible for God."

Mary said, "Behold, I am the handmaid of the Lord. May it be done to me according to your word." Then the angel departed from her.

During those days Mary set out and traveled to the hill country in haste to a town of Judah, where she entered the house of Zechariah and greeted Elizabeth.

LUKE 1:26–32, 34–40

MARY'S MOTHER

You know how all this ends; we didn't.
We only knew a girl was pregnant
Who shouldn't be,

And that girl was my daughter.

We're no different from you.
   I changed her diapers,
   She changed his.
   I taught her how to talk,
   She taught him.

We were supposed to take her to the graveyard,
Let everybody throw rocks at her until she's dead.
That's what the law says.

I was supposed to throw one myself
To show she deserved it.

Instead we sent her off to my cousin's.
She's a good girl. How could this happen?

It made lots of people mad.
You have to follow the law they said.
"Why should our daughters be virgins if yours isn't?"

"Yahweh never breaks the rules!" they said.
And who can argue?

But maybe that just goes to show
We don't always know what Yahweh's rules are.

It happened the way you heard.

It was the same with Sarah.
She started a whole tribe
After she was too old to get pregnant.

Yahweh is the one who makes life.
Who else?

And the way it happens isn't always the way
We think it's supposed to happen.

What if we knew
Exactly what God was supposed to do—
What would we need God for?

Sure it's hard to accept miracles,
But people do it all the time.

You have to forget the rules,
Do things you think you can't.

We all want it to be more normal,
More the way we understand.
More religious. You know,
So the priests can explain it.

I never got used to it.
"Why us?" I always wondered.

Why doesn't God pick somebody else?
Somebody who knows what's going on?
Somebody who's qualified?

It was the baby who got us through.
It wasn't his fault all this stuff happened.

When he got here we just loved him.
And held him close.

After that everything seemed to be ok.

That's why I always say, "Be gentle."
That's really all I have to say: be gentle.

You have to be tough.
You already know that or you wouldn't be here.

But be gentle.
That's what makes strong different than tough.

Women know this.
We learn it from our babies.

But the men,
It seems they have to learn it from the women.

part two

THE HOME

ome is where we live, where
we experience the events
of ordinary life. It is here
where we often least expect
to encounter Jesus, but as
we pay attention to the
events of our ordinary lives
we come to understand
how extraordinary they
often are.

The Father
of the Bride

This is anyone's father—a man who has spent his life working to provide for his family. But the fruits of his labor have often been taken from him by persons more powerful than he. As a result he is slightly stooped, from both his lifetime of manual labor and the lack of respect he has received. He wears workingman's clothing, and as he speaks he constantly looks down at his hands. His voice is soft, but firm.

THE BIBLICAL ACCOUNT
OF THE WEDDING IN CANA

On the third day there was a wedding in Cana in Galilee, and the mother of Jesus was there. Jesus and his disciples were also invited to the wedding.

When the wine ran short, the mother of Jesus said to him, "They have no wine." [And] Jesus said to her, "Woman, how does your concern affect me? My hour has not yet come." His mother said to the servers, "Do whatever he tells you."

Now there were six stone water jars there for Jewish ceremonial washings, each holding twenty to thirty gallons. Jesus told them, "Fill the jars with water." So they filled them to the brim. Then he told them, "Draw some out now and take it to the headwaiter." So they took it.

And when the headwaiter tasted the water that had become wine, without knowing where it came from (although the servers who had drawn the water knew), the headwaiter called the bridegroom and said to him, "Everyone serves good wine first, and then when people have drunk freely, an inferior one; but you have kept the good wine until now."

The Father of the Bride

What all this means I cannot say.
The arguments and theology
Are completely beyond me.

I knew him only as a wedding guest.
 It was my daughter's wedding,
 Surely the happiest day in any father's life.

But when I looked at the table nearly bare
Only my daughter's joy kept me there.

I had spent every cent I had
Or could borrow
And still there was only a single jar of wine,
And a few cakes.

 The cakes were thin and had no seeds on them
 And the wine was cheap and bitter.

Once the vineyard had been mine.
But the Romans had come you know,
With their quisling tax collectors,
And there was no longer anything we could call our own.

Our money went to Rome
To pay for fabulous orgies we could scarcely comprehend,
And I had no wine for my daughter's wedding.

 Politics do not interest me,
 But injustice, that is another thing.

He was part of our family
(His mother and mine are sisters)
And already his reputation for wisdom was great.

We had hoped he would somehow
Make our poor feast less painful.

The one thing they could not tax was our rabbi's words,
And the poorer we became
The more precious they were.

He agreed to join us,
To share our dancing, and our poverty.

We knew the wine could not last, so we drank sparingly,
But soon there was no more
And the celebration far from complete.

What he did then we do not know.
Only that suddenly there was wine without end,
And such wine as can never be described.

At first we thought he had purchased it.
Until we realized the quantity was too great,
And such wine cannot be bought, at any price.

As I said, all this I cannot explain.
  The chemistry is clearly impossible
  And the motive unclear.

Even I would not believe it had I seen it only with my eyes.

But the wine!
How can you argue with the wine?

I myself became drunk on it,
And my daughter long after spoke of it with great pride,
Thinking I had provided it.

Perhaps I should have told her.
Perhaps I have not been honest.

But there are things
Parents cannot tell their children,

Things they must learn for themselves,
As we learned them,
By drinking the wine at the wedding.

The
Roman Officer

The Roman officer is a professional soldier, someone accustomed to being in command and at home anywhere. It was through his skills, and the skills of others like him, that the ancient world had been unified politically. He is aware of this and takes his responsibilities seriously, but when he returns home he is a father and husband where he faces very different challenges. His clothing indicates high rank, but as he speaks it is clear this is a person who is much more than the uniform he wears. His voice conveys honesty, and he speaks slowly and with authority.

The Biblical Account
of the Healing of the Officer's Son

Now there was a royal official whose son was ill in Capernaum. When he heard that Jesus had arrived in Galilee from Judea, he went to him and asked him to come down and heal his son, who was near death.

Jesus said to him, "Unless you people see signs and wonders, you will not believe." The royal official said to him, "Sir, come down before my child dies."

Jesus said to him, "You may go; your son will live." The man believed what Jesus said to him and left.

While he was on his way back, his slaves met him and told him that his boy would live. He asked them when he began to recover. They told him, "The fever left him yesterday about one in the afternoon."

The father realized that just at that time Jesus had said to him, "Your son will live," and he and his whole household came to believe.

JOHN 4:46–53

THE ROMAN OFFICER

You may think these things quaint because they are old,
But there has never been anything quaint
About keeping peace in the Middle East.

When there is no one who speaks for everyone,
Everyone speaks for himself
And the result is endless bloodshed.

People dislike us. But had we not been here
Even greater injustice would have been done.

You envy us our power, I know.
But until you have held a sword in your hands
You have no idea how heavy it is.

Far from home, my children lived in an alien land,
Hated because I was feared.

The youngest grew ill simply from having no playmates.
(We provided him with servants, of course,
But they seemed only to make him lonelier.)

Even at night my wife and I lay far apart,
Divided by things we dared never discuss
For fear we would have to give them up.

We kept hearing of him, at a distance of course,
Always involved in the lives of others, principally the poor.
But when a child is dying no one is rich.

There is no power at the lip of the grave.

That is when I went to him.
You may say it was a desperate man's desperate act,
Or a father's love that knows no bounds.
    In either case I went.

Can you comprehend the cost? Walking down
The wretched alleys where I had so often marched my troops,
    Now alone and without a sword,
    Coming to ask a favor from one I had been sent to conquer.

He had every reason to laugh at me.
Why should he heal my son
When I had come to harm his people?

I had prepared my answer carefully—
I would treat him as an equal.

But when at last I reached him I found my plans irrelevant.
It was up to me whether my son would live or die, he said.
Then he looked into my eyes, past the medals,
Into a space I thought died when one became a man.

It was then I decided to follow him.

    Walking back,
    Past the miserable hovels of the poor,
    I saw things I had never seen before.
    Now that I was with him
    I was among them.

        When I arrived home I again buckled on my sword.
        It no longer seemed so heavy
        Now that my son had friends.

The Samaritan
Woman

Although the Samaritan woman has ended her childbearing days, her clothing reveals a last desperate effort to remain sexually attractive in hopes she can somehow find a place in a world she believes no longer wants her. She possesses a kind of animal vitality that sustains her and, although she no longer sees reason for hope, she constantly reaches out to those around her, even when they reject her. Her voice is husky but not powerful; she is physically strong but spiritually still a child. Her manner combines resignation with a refusal to entirely give up.

THE BIBLICAL ACCOUNT
OF THE SAMARITAN WOMAN

So he came to a town in Samaria called Sychar. . . . Jacob's well was there. Jesus, tired from his journey, sat down there at the well. It was about noon.

A woman of Samaria came to draw water. Jesus said to her, "Give me a drink. . . ." The Samaritan woman said to him, "How can you, a Jew, ask me, a Samaritan woman, for a drink?"

[And she began arguing with him.]

Jesus said to her, "Go call your husband and come back." The woman answered and said to him, "I do not have a husband."

Jesus answered her, "You are right in saying 'I do not have a husband.' For you have had five husbands, and the one you have now is not your husband. . . ."

At that moment his disciples returned, and were amazed that he was talking with a woman. . . .

The woman left her water jar and went into the town and said to the people, "Come see a man who told me everything I have done."

JOHN 4:5–9, 16–18, 27–29

THE SAMARITAN WOMAN

I doubt you know what it means to be a Samaritan
Or a woman alone at noon in the Middle East.
It's so hot you can hardly stand it.

I had to get my water then,
When the other women were at home with their husbands.
If they saw me coming they'd spit on the path,
Make me walk over it.

I was sitting there all alone that day,
Watching the paint peeling off the cracked plaster
And the flowers wilting on a dying vine.
Scuffing the dirt with my worn-out shoes.

What do you do with a life that's over
Before you're dead?
    You wake up in the morning,
    All you can see in the mirror are holes.

What a difference having breasts makes.
Breaking rules is something only a man's supposed to do,
Like fighting wars, or having money.

A woman does something and she's not human anymore.
What she is I don't know, some sort of monster maybe,
Somebody the good women can tell their daughters,
"Don't be like that."

    They all thought I was a traitor. But I was just lonely.
    ("Just," I say, as if lonely doesn't matter. But what else is there?)

71

Everybody looks down on us Samaritans.
The big shots in Jerusalem say we don't do things right.

So when he starts talking to me I start arguing with him.
    "I'm a bad woman from a bad town," I tell him.
    "Leave me alone."

    I don't want him to know who I am.
    I've had enough people tell me I'm worthless,
    I don't need anymore.

But he won't give up,
Talking to me like I was family.
And he asks me for a drink! Like I was his sister or something.

The longer we talked the more I could see
He knew more about me than I did,
That he liked me even if he knew who I was.

    I had thought there were things that could never be told:
    The secrets of the bed and the heart
    We take to the grave unsaid.

    But with him
    There wasn't anything you needed to be ashamed of,
    So long as you told the truth.

That's when I ran back to town, telling everybody,
"You don't need to be afraid anymore!"

    And everybody came out, like it was a wedding.
    We kept him with us for three days,
    And after that we quit telling lies.

The
Artist

The artist is memorable above all for her hair. It is long and flowing, bright red, a fountain of warmth flowing from within. When she enters a room she immediately begins to inspect its furnishings, especially the wall hangings. She is interested in very different things than the Roman official, whom she knows. As she speaks she holds a small piece of sculpture in her hands, and looks inward. Her voice is firm but not assertive. Her clothing indicates quiet good taste.

THE BIBLICAL ACCOUNT
OF THE ANOINTING AT BETHANY

When he was in Bethany . . . a woman came with an alabaster jar of perfumed oil, costly genuine spikenard. She broke the alabaster jar and poured it on his head.

There were some who were indignant. "Why has there been this waste of perfumed oil? It could have been sold for more than three hundred days' wages and the money given to the poor." They were infuriated with her.

Jesus said, "Let her alone. Why do you make trouble for her? She has done a good thing for me. The poor you will always have with you, and whenever you wish you can do good to them, but you will not always have me.

"She has done what she could."

THE ARTIST

All I had were the precious oils,
Pressed from a thousand flowers long ago.
My teacher gave them to me when he died.

It's all I had. I didn't have anything else.
And you had to do something.
You couldn't just pretend nothing had happened.

The good people thought I should have sold it.
They wanted the money.
They could use it for something worthwhile, they said.

But how could they understand?
Some things you can't buy
Or sell.

He understood.
That's why I'm here.
Although I was terribly suspicious at first.

Religious people have never treated me well.
They want us to decorate their temples
For cheap,

Then go away.
They love art, sort of. But they hate artists.
I don't know why.

When I saw he wasn't afraid I started crying.
Just weeping. Like a baby.
Getting his feet all wet.

I tried fixing it up with my hair,
But it didn't make much difference.
You can't change much with just your hair.

I felt like a fool but I couldn't quit.
And he kept saying, "It's ok, it's ok,
Don't stop."

It's hard to put something like that in words,
But you could understand what he was saying
With the part of you that doesn't have words.

You knew it was the right thing,
The way artists know what other people like.

It's hard to explain.

It's the same way the poor understand.
They know from all that pain
What really matters.

But the rich . . .
The rich just don't get it.
If they did they wouldn't be rich.

The Man Possessed

This man's movements indicate he has only recently entered ordinary human society. He is ill at ease and his body is covered with the marks left by his years as a homeless person. There are still cuts, bruises, and ragged scars on his arms and face, and his skin is like leather from living unprotected in the outdoors for many years. The way he wears his clothing suggests his recent nudity, and he is not quite sure where he should sit. His voice conveys the calm amazement appropriate to someone who has just experienced a miracle.

The Biblical Account
of the Healing of the Gerasene Demoniac

When he got out of the boat, at once a man from the tombs who had an unclean spirit met him. The man had been dwelling among the tombs, and no one could restrain him any longer, even with a chain. . . . Night and day among the tombs and on the hillsides he was always crying out and bruising himself with stones.

Catching sight of Jesus from a distance, he ran up and prostrated himself before him, crying out in a loud voice, "What have you to do with me, Jesus, Son of the Most High God? I adjure you by God, do not torment me." (He had been saying to him, "Unclean spirit, come out of the man!")

He asked him, "What is your name?" He replied, "Legion is my name. There are many of us." And he pleaded earnestly with him not to drive them away from that territory. . . .

They pleaded with him, "Send us into the swine. Let us enter them." And he let them, and . . . the herd of about two thousand rushed down a steep bank into the sea, where they were drowned.

The swineherds ran away and reported the incident . . . [and] people came out to see what had happened. As they approached Jesus, they caught sight of the man who had been possessed by Legion, sitting there clothed and in his right mind. . . . Then they began to beg him to leave their district.

As he was getting into the boat, the man who had been possessed pleaded to remain with him. But . . . [Jesus] told him, "Go home to your family and announce to them all that the Lord in his pity has done for you."

MARK 5:2–19

THE MAN POSSESSED

You call it "mental illness" now.
But what have your labels to do with pain,
Except hide it? Like a bandage with no salve.

When they take over, they take your life.
You do things nobody would ever choose.

I'd wake up in the gutter,
My face smeared with donkey dung,
My tongue dripping slime.

You think I chose this?

When people couldn't ignore me anymore,
They'd lock me up. But it never works.
The demons can overpower anybody's good intentions.

When we choose not to choose,
Our souls get filled with things we can't control.

It has to do with power,
What we can do and what we can't do.
That's where we're all mixed up.

Everybody thinks he's in charge.
But it's all a dream. We just live here.
The only question is who we work for.

Nobody wants to be like this.
But how can you change what you are with what you are?

When he came I found out you can be free.
Not because the demons left me,
But because now I lived where they had.

If you don't live in your soul,
Somebody else will.
And how can you be free then?

When he left us I wanted to go along,
But he told me to stay behind,
Tell people what I learned.

So I tell everybody I can,

    Nothing God made is evil;
    Evil is the gifts we have refused.

    Had we accepted them,
    We would not need to steal.

Martha
of Bethany

Martha is the gracious hostess, concerned above all with making people comfortable in her home. As she speaks she constantly moves about, tidying up things with great efficiency, wiping away the dust. She is wearing an apron and there is a scarf on her head. Her motto is "Get the work done first, then you can sit down and talk." Although there is a worried look on her face, she is not compulsive; she genuinely wants things to be as nice as possible for her family and her guests. Her voice is strong and practical.

The Biblical Account of Mary, Martha, and Lazarus

He entered a village where a woman whose name was Martha welcomed him. She had a sister named Mary [who] sat beside the Lord at his feet listening to him speak. Martha, burdened with much serving, said, "Lord, do you not care that my sister has left me by myself to do the serving? Tell her to help me."

The Lord said to her in reply, "Martha, Martha, you are anxious and worried about many things. There is need of only one thing. Mary has chosen the better part and it will not be taken from her."

[Later Martha and Mary's brother Lazarus falls ill. The sisters send for Jesus, but before he arrives their brother dies and is buried.]

When Martha heard that Jesus was coming, she went to meet him; but Mary sat at home. Martha said to Jesus, "Lord, if you had been here, my brother would not have died. . . ."

She went and called her sister Mary secretly, saying, "The teacher is here and is asking for you." As soon as [Mary] heard this, she rose quickly and went to him. . . .

Jesus said, "Take away the stone." Martha . . . said to him, "Lord, by now there will be a stench; he has been dead for four days." Jesus said to her, "Did I not tell you that if you believe you will see the glory of God?" . . .

The dead man came out, tied hand and foot with burial bands, and his face was wrapped in a cloth. So Jesus said to them, "Untie him and let him go."

MARTHA OF BETHANY

We were stuck until he came.

Our parents left us a home but no life.
We had everything, and nothing.
A past with no future, riches without joy.

It was like being buried alive.
Everybody with a knife at somebody else's throat.
You couldn't move.

We all just went inside and peeked through the curtains.
You couldn't talk to your neighbors or anybody.
They might ask you for something.

Everybody put up bars, hoarded food, waited to die.
We thought it was the Romans, but really it was fear in charge.
Always there, like an animal behind your back.

Then he walked through the door.

You'll never know what it's like until he comes to your house.
He acts like an old friend
Even when you've never seen him before.
And pretty soon you start acting that way too.

You have to do something, either talk to him or throw him out.
If you talk to him your whole life changes.

    And if you throw him out where are you?
    Back in the same old rut,
    All alone and nothing to do.

I wanted to have it both ways at first,
Talk to him and not change.
My sister dropped everything, listened to him by the hour.
"What if everybody did that!" I yelled at her.

But then my brother died and everything changed.

He was hiding in the desert.
(They were trying to kill him.)
But we told him Lazarus is dying and he came.
He risked his life to come help us.

"You're too late," I told him.
"We already buried him."
But I was wrong.

I can't explain it, but it happened.
My brother was dead. We buried him.
And then he came walking out of the tomb.

That's when I understood.
The way we were living was like that,
Scared to death because we think what we can see
Is all there is to see.

    And I started listening too.
    Like Mary.

    If you want a nice house,
    You've got to start on the inside.

The Man
Born Blind

This man, who was born without sight, now has eyes that are in constant motion, looking about him at everything, trying to make up for all he missed when he was blind. Color especially fascinates him. As he speaks he constantly reaches out to touch things, as he did when he was blind. His clothing places him among the common people, as does his speech. His voice is filled with a calm awe. He is genuinely surprised at the questions people ask him.

The Biblical Account
of the Man Born Blind

As he passed by he saw a man blind from birth. His disciples asked him, "Rabbi, who sinned, this man or his parents, that he was born blind?" Jesus answered, "Neither he nor his parents sinned; it is so that the works of God might be made visible through him. . . ."

He spat on the ground, made clay with the saliva, smeared the clay on his eyes, and said to him, "Go wash in the Pool of Siloam." (which means Sent.) So he went and washed, and came back able to see.

His neighbors and those who had seen him earlier as a beggar said, "Isn't this the one who used to sit and beg?" Some said, "It is," but others said, "No, he just looks like him." He said, "I am."

So they said to him, "[So] how were your eyes opened?" He replied, "The man called Jesus made clay and anointed my eyes and told me, 'Go to Siloam and wash.' So I went there and washed and was able to see. . . ."

[The religious authorities] called the man . . . and said to him, . . . "We know this man is a sinner."

He replied, "If he is a sinner, I do not know. One thing I do know is that I was blind and now I see."

JOHN 9:1–3, 6–11, 24–25

THE MAN BORN BLIND

You have no notion what darkness is,
You whose eyes are closed only when you choose.
But my eyes had never seen light
Until that day he touched them, and they came alive.

I remember my parents arguing long into the night—
Whose fault it was. And why?
What had they done to deserve this?
Thinking I was asleep.

But for the blind, night and day are very much alike
And their words have lived to this day,
Like a rock in my shoe.

Whose fault?
That is the question we had struggled with so long.
Endless arguments and never an answer.

Of course we had heard of him,
But thinking our case hopeless, ignored him.
What could he do for someone so cursed?

We went on with our usual pursuits.
    I sitting in the streets begging,
    A pitiful sight living on pity,
    While my parents brooded about the kitchen table,
    Shamed beyond words.

It was his disciples who saw me,
Starting yet another argument,
As though blindness also made me deaf and invisible.

I had heard it all a thousand times before.
The religious have always treated me as a problem
To be solved.

But he seemed uninterested in their debates.
That was when the unthinkable happened.

There was a warm stirring in my eyes
And a kind voice saying,
"Go, wash the mud from your eyes."

My first sight was the water.
The joy I experienced
Cannot be described.

Thinking my blindness a curse,
It never occurred to anyone I might be healed.

    Afterwards
    People asked me to explain.

    It seemed so strange to ask "Why?"
    When one can see.

St. Peter's
Wife

St. Peter's wife is an older woman who possesses real power. Her responsibility is to make certain her family succeeds, and she takes this task very seriously. It is due to her success, and that of other women like her, that the human race has survived. She is dressed in an apron and her hair is tied back. As she speaks she moves about the room, rearranging the furniture and projecting an image of great efficiency and common sense. She speaks bluntly, with pauses between her thoughts.

The Biblical Account
of the call of the First Disciples
and the Cure of Simon's Mother-in-Law

As he passed by the Sea of Galilee, he saw Simon and his brother Andrew casting their nets into the sea; they were fishermen. Jesus said to them, "Come after me, and I will make you fishers of men." Then they abandoned their nets and followed him.

He walked along a little farther and saw James, the son of Zebedee, and his brother John. They too were in a boat mending their nets. Then he called them. So they left their father Zebedee in the boat along with the hired men and followed him.

Then they came to Capernaum, and on the sabbath he entered the synagogue and taught. The people were astonished at his teaching, for he taught them as one having authority and not as the scribes. . . .

On leaving the synagogue he entered the house of Simon and Andrew with James and John.

Simon's mother-in-law lay sick with a fever. They immediately told him about her. He approached, grasped her hand, and helped her up. Then the fever left her and she waited on them.

Mark 1:16–22; 29–31

St. Peter's Wife

When a woman gives herself she doesn't keep anything.
If you do there's nothing left for anybody.
But it's not easy being married to a saint.

It never was easy being married to Peter.
Once he made up his mind, he was like a rock.
Hard to get along with, but you could always depend on him.

Until he changed all the sudden.
Not overnight mind you. Nobody ever does.
It took some time, but he wasn't the same.

Sometimes I wondered,
Is the man I married still sleeping in my bed?
(He always did snore. That stayed the same.)

We weren't wealthy, but we were comfortable.
Enough to eat. A roof over our heads.
Clothes for the kids.

Peter always caught fish, if anybody did.
And I took good care of what we had.
Nothing got wasted in my house.

But just when we were getting ahead
He'd come home at night empty-handed.
He'd been listening to some new rabbi, he said.

I'd cook us a meal from what I'd saved up, not saying a word,
And Peter would still be talking about this rabbi
Way past the kids' bedtime.

I don't mind telling you we had some bitter words those days.
I'd say, I'm keeping my end of the bargain and you're not.
And he'd say, what do you know about religion and politics,
I don't tell you how to run the house.

You won't believe this but Peter and his buddies had big plans.
Some crazy scheme where this rabbi was gonna be king
And they'd all be his chief honchos.

No wonder the Romans thought we were fools.
What'd they think they'd do when the soldiers came,
Read from the Torah?

Sometimes Peter would bring him to the house
    and I'd feed them both.
Nobody ever said I wasn't a good wife.
But they knew how I felt.

Sure the country had problems with the Romans.
But what could we do?
The only swords we had were old ones.
Nothing compared to what the Romans had.

Every time we tried to fight back they just sent more soldiers
And it was worse than before.
Peter and his buddies weren't the first ones with these ideas.

It was my mother that changed my mind.
When she saw Peter and me going apart
She didn't want to live anymore.

    Every month you could see her getting closer to the end.
    I don't mind telling you it was a bad time.

Of course she took my side. She always did.
But she saw something I didn't.
We never talked about it, we never had time.
Too busy with the house and the kids.

I know people die. I know you have to say goodbye.
But this is the worst it'd ever been.

When you have to live with no mother
You find out real quick being tough's not enough.

Well, you know the rest,
How he came to our house that Sabbath day.
We all thought she was dying when he came.

He talked for just a minute,
I don't know what they said.
But all a sudden she was her old self again.

    Outta bed, on her feet,
    Helping people like she used to.
    Feeling needed.

And the children!
They started acting different.
Playing house, chasing the other kids around the lake.
Jumping rope.

It was like we all came back to life.
Even the neighbors just watching.
I can't explain it, I don't have words like some.

    But you don't need words if you watch what people do.

After that Peter and me,
We followed him together.

It wasn't easy.
The Romans got him. Like I knew they would.
But then . . . well, you know what happened.

Who could ever turn back after that?

They put Peter in jail for a while.
But an angel got him out.
You don't forget that either.

That's when we went to Rome.
A couple a hicks from the sticks moving to the Big Apple . . .
How we did it I'll never know.

We helped each other, I know that.
And he was with us, that's for sure.

The bad part came when the church split.
That's when they got Peter.
The same way they got the Master back home.

It hurt terrible seeing him die. And Paul too.
But I wasn't alone anymore.
And pretty soon I joined them.

    It was a good life.

part three

THE TEMPLE

The temple is where we go to worship. It is here that our fundamental values are formed and affirmed—and changed. Those who come to Jesus expecting their existing beliefs to be affirmed are virtually always disappointed. The religious leaders of his own time were his greatest opponents.

The Rich
Young Man

This young man has obviously inherited
great wealth. There is a large gold chain
around his neck, and he is wearing
expensive shoes and designer clothes.
However, he is not ostentatious about his
wealth. He regards it his by right—
something due him in the natural order
of things—and he genuinely wants to be
a good person, someone who does all the
right things. As he tells his story he
wanders about trying to find a place to sit,
but finally leaves with his shoulders
hunched and his hands in his pockets.

As he was setting out on a journey, a man ran up, knelt down before him, and asked him, "Good teacher, what must I do to inherit eternal life?"

Jesus answered him, "Why do you call me good? No one is good but God alone. You know the commandments: 'You shall not kill; you shall not commit adultery; you shall not steal; you shall not bear false witness; you shall not defraud; honor your father and your mother.'"

He replied and said to him, "Teacher, all of these I have observed from my youth."

Jesus, looking at him, loved him and said to him, "You are lacking in one thing. Go, sell what you have, and give to [the] poor and you will have treasure in heaven; then come, follow me."

At that statement his face fell, and he went away sad, for he had many possessions.

MARK 10:17–22

THE RICH YOUNG MAN

I came to him weary,
Having tried everything.

It was a long walk to where he was
And I was exhausted when I arrived.

The journey hardly seemed worthwhile
When finally I found him
Sitting at table with many unsavory characters.

He looked at me and saw what I wanted,
Then turned away to a beggar who had no legs.
    I had to wait my turn, and would have gone away
    Had there been anywhere else to go.

When finally it came my turn,
He looked into my well-fed face

Past the superficial pain with which I mask my self,
Into the space where our souls reside.

I had come to debate but his eyes saw
Things that are beyond debate.

He said nothing at first. Nor did I.
Only the silence spoke.

And when he opened his mouth
It was only to say what we already knew:

    There is no road from where I was
    To where he is.

It was as Solzhenitsyn has said,
I would have been glad then had someone else, with power,
Stripped me bare,

Taken the gold chains from me,
And the credit cards,
Given me no choice but to be poor.

But he made me choose
And I found one cannot choose to be poor.

"Take everything you have
And give it to the poor," he said.

And I knew then he understood wealth
As I thought only the wealthy do,
And that understanding is what must be given.

You will understand the pain I carried with me
From that meeting.

    To be rich
    And yet to have to teach the poor to be rich:

    That is more than I was prepared to give
    When I came to ask him for something
    That was very important
    To me.

The Syrian
Dancing Girl

The Syrian dancing girl is young and sexual, bounding into the room filled with apparently unlimited energy, and communicating primarily with her body—reaching out to us with her hands as she speaks. For her the body is primary, and her clothing clearly indicates a commitment to the erotic, without being vulgar. She has no concern for propriety; she is what she is and sees no reason to pretend otherwise. Her voice is the voice of the street; this is a girl who "has a mouth."

THE BIBLICAL ACCOUNT
OF JESUS EATING WITH SINNERS

While he was at table in [Levi's] house, many tax collectors and sinners sat with Jesus and his disciples; for there were many who followed him.

Some scribes who were Pharisees saw that he was eating with sinners and tax collectors and said to his disciples, "Why does he eat with tax collectors and sinners?"

Jesus heard this and said to them [that], "Those who are well do not need a physician, but the sick do. I do not come to call the righteous but sinners."

They are like children who sit in the marketplace and call to one another,

> *"We played the flute for you, but you did not dance.*
> *We sang a dirge, but you did not weep."*

For John the Baptist came neither eating food nor drinking wine, and you said, "He is possessed by a demon." The Son of Man came eating and drinking and you said, "Look, he is a glutton and a drunkard, a friend of tax collectors and sinners."

MARK 2:15–17; LUKE 7:32–34

THE SYRIAN DANCING GIRL

Hey you guys, this is too gloomy!
All you religious people talk about is death and dying.
You're so busy bein' good you don't have time to live.
Why so sad all the time?

You wanna know what fun is? Go to a wedding he's at.
I can't remember everything he said,
But I sure remember he danced with me.

Sure I want a go to heaven, but what's wrong with this life?
I'll tell you what's wrong with it:
Nobody ever *does* anything.

And I don't mean gettin' drunk and actin' crazy
So you feel all crummy afterwards.
This was different. You wanted to do it again.

You think it's awful, I know, him touchin' me.
So did our good people.
Well, let me tell you, they're the ones he can't stand.

No wonder you're so sad, thinkin' he's just like you.
I know some people have to be miserable to be happy.
Into whips and handcuffs, you know, tyin' people up.

But he wasn't like that.
He wanted to dance with everybody.
I mean everybody!

    He woulda danced with them but they won't dance.

Hey, it's no big deal.
Shake your booty or turn into a prune.
Why you so afraid of your bodies?
You think the devil made 'em?

You talk about lovin' God
But you're really mad at somethin'.
I don't know what.

You ask me,
Good's just a phony word for phony.

He wasn't good, he was better than that.
That night he came to our house
I asked him why he was different.

He told me good's what you do,
You know, to make people happy.
Not not doin' all the stuff you're afraid of.

Afterwards I went back to dancin' at the tavern.
The drums was playin' like always, *"Dum Dum Dum,"*
But they don't sound like they did before.
And I starts thinkin', is this the way it's supposed to be?

And I walks into the temple where I never was before.
And I hears the choir singin' so sweet.

And I starts to wonder,
Is there any place here for me?

Nicodemus

Nicodemus is wearing clerical garb,
including a large black hat creased down
the center that nearly covers his eyes. He is
accustomed to being in charge in the
religious world, and walks about with his
hands clasped behind his back, looking for
a place in Jesus' world. His voice is the one
he uses in the pulpit, deep and sonorous,
but caring at the same time, revealing real
humanity beneath his formality and sense
of responsibility.

THE BIBLICAL ACCOUNT
OF THE VISIT OF NICODEMUS

Now there was a Pharisee named Nicodemus, a ruler of the Jews. He came to Jesus at night and said to him, "Rabbi, we know that you are a teacher who has come from God, for no one can do these signs that you are doing unless God is with him."

Jesus answered and said to him, "Amen, amen, I say to you, no one can see the kingdom of God without being born from above."

Nicodemus said to him, "How can a person once grown old be born again? Surely he cannot reenter his mother's womb and be born again, can he?"

Jesus answered, "Amen, amen, I say to you, no one can enter the kingdom of God without being born of water and Spirit. What is born of flesh is flesh and what is born of spirit is spirit.

"Do not be amazed that I told you, 'You must be born from above.' The wind blows where it wills, and you can hear the sound it makes, but you do not know where it comes from or where it goes; so it is with everyone who is born of the Spirit."

Nicodemus answered and said to him, "How can this happen?" Jesus answered and said to him, "You are the teacher of Israel and you do not understand this?"

NICODEMUS

It's hard to change.
You live behind walls all these years, afraid to go out,
Protecting your reputation—so hard to achieve, so easy to lose.

Only at night could I visit him,
And even then I had to hide my face.
My hand was trembling when I knocked at his door.

Religion was our great treasure,
And my duty was to preserve it—
To enforce conformity, to punish those who did not obey,
Severely if necessary.

His words were very powerful,
Everyone agreed.

And what he said did not itself seem dangerous,
But there was nothing to make rules from.

Having taught all my life
Religion is doing things one would not choose,
This was difficult to accept.

"How is this possible?" I asked him that night.
We are what we are, it can't be changed.
The best we can do is follow the rules.

But he only shook his head
And asked how a religious teacher
Could know so little about the inner life.

The real is more than the visible, he said.
Like the wind,
Everyone feels it but no one can see it.

Our souls are like boats, he said,
Journeying an infinite ocean to an unknown goal.

When the wind blows we must go where it goes
Or else drop anchor and forever fight it
With only our will as the weapon.

Truth has a force
Like the wind on the ocean
Which can neither be seen nor resisted.

But how can you control what you can't understand?
There has to be something the people can obey.

Otherwise there'll be dancing in the streets,
No respect for the better classes!

Not wishing to take such a risk,
I covered my face
And walked back through the night

To my office.

The
Prodigal Son

The prodigal son is dressed plainly, but not noticeably so. The hard life he once led has left its marks on his face, but he is now a person at peace, and we find pleasure in being with him. His story is the one he once told Jesus, when for the first time it made sense. His voice is firm and mature, filled with wonder and gratitude at what has happened, but also with sorrow at his brother's anger.

THE BIBLICAL PARABLE OF THE LOST SON

A man had two sons, and the younger son said to his father, "Father, give me the share of your estate that should come to me. . . ." After a few days, the younger son collected all his belongings and set off to a distant country where he squandered his inheritance.

When he had freely spent everything, a severe famine struck, . . . so he hired himself out to one of the local citizens who sent him to his farm to tend the swine. And he longed to eat his fill of the pods on which the swine fed, but nobody gave him any.

Coming to his senses he thought, "How many of my father's hired workers have more than enough food to eat, but here am I, dying from hunger. I shall get up and go to my father and I shall say to him, 'Father, . . . I no longer deserve to be called your son; treat me as you would treat one of your hired workers. . . .'"

While he was still a long way off, his father caught sight of him, and was filled with compassion. He ran to his son, embraced him and kissed him. His son said to him, "Father, I have sinned against heaven and against you; I no longer deserve to be called your son."

But his father ordered his servants, "Quickly bring the finest robe and put it on him; put a ring on his finger and sandals on his feet. . . . Then let us celebrate with a feast, because this son of mine was dead, and has come to life again. . . ."

Now the older son had been out in the field and, on his way back, as he neared the house, he heard the sound of music and dancing. He called one of the servants and asked him what this might mean. The servant said to him, "Your brother has returned. . . ."

He became angry, and when he refused to enter the house, his father came out and pleaded with him. . . .

Luke 15:11–32

THE PRODIGAL SON

It was a long way home.
I had forgotten the way,
And my mind was still mushy from the wine.

My loins seemed empty.
Partly it was the infection,
And partly it was that I had eaten nothing.

I was like a dead man walking,
My feet disconnected from my legs,
And I knew I would never dance again.

    At night I slept under the bridges
    And in the morning begged food
    From those I once thought poor.

The road ran south
To the valley where my father lives,
But I had no shoes and the rocks in the ruts were jagged.

    I found promise can make pain bearable
    But cannot make it less.

The greatest pain of all was the shame.

As I neared my father's house I hid in the ditches,
Unwilling to show my face,
Until I realized no one knew me anymore.

But still I traveled at night,
For my father is very wealthy, and known to be so,
And what excuse has a son of his to travel the roads in rags?

Arriving at last, I hid in a cave for many days,
Unwilling, I thought, to cause him pain.

Until nearly starved, and fearful of discovery,
I took my shame like a sack of rocks
And went to one of my father's servants.

I tried to explain, and he tried to listen but could not.
I think I had never before seen tears of joy.
They are more copious, and cleansing,
Like rivers fed from mountain snows.

"Your father will be so happy," he said.
And again I tried to explain: I no longer deserved a father,
That I had come home to be a slave, not a son.

But he seemed not to hear.
"You must go home," he said.

When I explained I no longer had a home,
That I had squandered everything my father had given me,
He looked away, through the door.

"Look," he said.
And when I did, saw my father,
a man on old legs, running.

It was then I was forced to choose.
The sack of rocks I had carried, more than a thousand miles,
Slept with at night like a lover. Or . . .

I left them there, in the servant's house
(What he did with them I've never known)
And ran, again a child to his father.

I wanted to fall on my face, but he would not have it.
"Already you have fallen far enough," he said,
And made me stand on my feet so he could embrace me.

"I had thought there were no tears left," he said softly.
Then looked at me with a love
That made my rags seem almost obscene.

"I must change before I go home," I said, looking down.
But he, asserting the prerogative of the parent,
Took me home as I was,

> Bathed me in clean water,
> Gave me a new robe to wear, trimmed in red,
> And afterward a great banquet.

In the end it was my brother, the one who had worked so hard,
Who caused our father the greatest pain.
He was angry, and let it be known.
Never had such attention been paid him,
And surely he had earned it.

Strange as it may seem, I envied him.
How comforting it would be to deserve all this,
To think it yours by right, as dividends are paid by IBM.

> All I could tell him was this,

> > My riches are all gifts,
> > Given me despite my having asked
> > For what I deserved.

The Former Pharisee

This woman is prim and proper, the very model of respectability and common sense. She has reached the time when it is clear her life was wasted—for her the greatest possible tragedy—but her great strength of character enables her to bear even this. Although she is profoundly unhappy she is not bitter, and there is no trace of self-pity in either her voice or manner. Her dress is sensible and a bit severe, and her voice matter of fact and to the point. She stands close to the doorway as she speaks, having only recently come into the room where she speaks.

THE BIBLICAL ACCOUNT
OF THE DENUNCIATION OF THE PHARISEES

A Pharisee invited him to dine at his home. He entered and reclined at table to eat. The Pharisee was amazed to see that he did not observe the prescribed washing before the meal.

The Lord said to him, "Oh you Pharisees! Although you cleanse the outside of the cup and the dish, inside you are filled with plunder and evil.

"You fools! Did not the maker of the outside also make the inside? But as to what is within, give alms, and behold, everything will be clean for you.

"Woe to you Pharisees! You pay tithes of mint and of rue and of every garden herb, but you pay no attention to judgment and to love for God. . . .

"Woe to you Pharisees! You love the seat of honor in synagogues and greetings in marketplaces. Woe to you! You are like unseen graves over which people unknowingly walk."

When he left, the scribes and Pharisees began to act with hostility toward him. . . . Meanwhile, so many people were crowding together that they were trampling one another underfoot.

He began to speak, first to his disciples, "Beware of the leaven—that is, the hypocrisy—of the Pharisees. There is nothing concealed that will not be revealed, nor secret that will not be known."

LUKE 11:37–44; 11:53–12:2

THE FORMER PHARISEE

My story is sad. I tried to make it happy,
But things don't always turn out as we think they should.

He confused us, the ones who tried the hardest.
We thought sin was the problem and morality the answer,
But he didn't think our sins were that important.

I couldn't stand it.
I knew the wicked make fun,
But when the holy start shaking their heads,
How can you stand that?

Let's face it, it's scary out there.
And without any rules,
What'd he want us to do?
Run around naked, let everybody see everything?

What kind of a place would that be?
There are some things you just don't talk about.

That's why we turned on him like an enemy.
He was worse than the Romans, we decided.
Who wants to be free if you haven't earned it?

But then I started seeing
The ones with him were happier than I,
And I started thinking, maybe you really could live that way.

   I knew the rules don't really matter that much,
   But I kept them anyway. It made me feel good,
   Especially when I knew the others weren't.

But still I didn't know for sure.
I wanted to wait until everything was settled.
Better safe than sorry, I always said.

He kept saying, "Follow me,"
And I'd say, "I'll think about it."
I wanted to know where I'd end up before I started out.

Every day there was another reason to be afraid,
Until finally I used up my whole life playing it safe.
Then you find out it's all been a big waste.

Let me tell you, he was right.
You can't live two lives—
One people can see, and one just you know about.

> We thought we were so holy,
> But all we were doing was covering up our sins
> With a coat of pious paint.

The only way that works is his way.
Don't worry about you and whether you're right,
Worry about what other people need.

> By the time I caught on it was too late.
> I hardly had anything left to give.

> > It's for the gifts we give
> > That people remember us,
> > Not the rules we keep.

> > That's why nobody knows my name.

Thomas
the Doubter

Thomas is wiry and intense. He paces as he speaks, rubbing his head and often looking down at the floor. He is ashamed of his past, and at the same time aware his mistakes have greatly enriched human history. His voice indicates a person whose opinions are firmly held, but whose natural tendency is to doubt rather than be dogmatic. He cares very much about telling the truth. His clothing is that of a worker whose job is finished for the day.

On the evening of that first [Easter], when the doors were locked where the disciples were, . . . Jesus came and stood in their midst and said to them, "Peace be with you."

When he had said this, he showed them his hands and his side. The disciples rejoiced when they saw the Lord. [Jesus] said to them again, "Peace be with you. As the Father has sent me, so I send you." And when he had said this, he breathed on them and said to them, "Receive the holy Spirit. . . ."

Thomas, called Didymus, one of the Twelve, was not with them when Jesus came. So the other disciples said to him, "We have seen the Lord." But he said to them, "Unless I see the mark of the nails in his hands and put my finger into the nailmarks and put my hand into his side, I will not believe."

Now a week later his disciples were again inside and Thomas was with them. Jesus came, although the doors were locked, and stood in their midst and said, "Peace be with you."

Then he said to Thomas, "Put your finger here and see my hands, and bring your hand and put it into my side, and do not be unbelieving, but believe."

Thomas answered, "My Lord and my God!"

John 20:19–28

Thomas the Doubter

You never know for sure.
People say what they want to hear all the time.

Half the people are full of it,
The other half are liars.

    I know that's not true,
    But it's what I used to say.

Look, the reason we followed him was
We thought we knew where he was going.

We all believed we'd found this great leader—
He'd make us rich and powerful, if we got in good with him.

But then he died.
Didn't even put up a fight.

I told myself never again—
Believe some crazy dream.
Once is bad enough. You don't do it twice.

So when they said he was still alive I laughed.
From now on I trust my eyes, I said, not my heart.

Put yourself in my place, I'm no different than you.
Whatever is, is. You can't change it.

But then he came back to me. In person.
And I discovered doubt won't save you.

Frankly I never was that religious.
Not anti, don't get me wrong,
But Jesus didn't pick other rabbis for his disciples.

We were mostly fishermen,
And you don't catch fish saying your prayers.

We weren't looking for some escape from life—
We wanted a life.

Our mistake was we thought we knew what that was.

    Life wasn't what we expected,
    But what we expected didn't work
    So it had to be something else.

    I don't know why we couldn't see it.

You end up so busy making sure you're right
You can't see what's right in front of you.

You end up being a fool
Trying not to be one.

        Ever since then I've always wondered,

        Why is it we doubters
        Never doubt our own doubts?

Cleopas's Wife

A simple, plain woman, much like a thousand others, we know her only as Cleopas's wife, who lived in a small village outside Jerusalem. In a crowd she was invisible, and in fact people often forgot she was present, even when they were in the same room. It was this woman who served a meal to the stranger her husband had invited to their home that first Easter Sunday. She is dressed as a housewife, and speaks quietly but with a sense of her importance as food provider. She is setting the table for yet another meal as she speaks.

THE BIBLICAL ACCOUNT
OF THE APPEARANCE ON THE ROAD TO EMMAUS

That very day two of them were going to a village seven miles from Jerusalem called Emmaus. . . . And it happened that while they were conversing and debating, Jesus himself drew near and walked with them, but their eyes were prevented from recognizing him.

He asked them, "What are you discussing as you walk along?" They stopped, looking downcast. One of them, named Cleopas, said to him, "Are you the only visitor to Jerusalem who does not know of the things that have taken place there in these days?"

And he replied, "What sort of things?" They said, "The things that happened to Jesus the Nazarene, who was a prophet mighty in deed and word, how our chief priests and rulers both handed him over and crucified him. But we were hoping that he would be the one to redeem Israel;" and besides all this, it is now the third day since this took place. Some women from our group, however, have astounded us: they were at the tomb early in the morning and did not find his body; they came back and reported . . . he was alive. . . ."

And he said to them, "Oh, how foolish you are! How slow of heart to believe all that the prophets spoke! Was it not necessary that the Messiah should suffer these things and enter into his glory?" . . .

As they approached the village . . . he gave the impression that he was going on farther. But they urged him, "Stay with us, for it is nearly evening and the day is almost over." So he went in to stay with them. And . . . while he was with them at table, he took bread, said the blessing, broke it, and gave it to them. With that their eyes were opened and they recognized him. . . .

So they set out at once and returned to Jerusalem where they . . . recounted what had taken place on the way and how he was made known to them in the breaking of the bread.

LUKE 24:13-35

CLEOPAS'S WIFE

We were just ordinary people,
Living in an ordinary house, in an ordinary village.
Until he came.

We'd given up. What can you do
When they can kill anybody anytime they want to?
Sometimes it seemed like we were alive but not really living.

He gave us such hope. Then they killed him too.
We thought it was all over,
That there wasn't anything you could do
Except hide and hope they didn't get you too.

    You don't know how scared we were.
    It was all we talked about.

And then he came back from the grave.

I know you think that's impossible. So did we.
Even when he walked into my house and sat down at my table
I never dreamed it was him.

Why we didn't recognize him I really can't say.
We knew what he looked like.
Just the week before we all went to Jerusalem to see him.

Everybody was there for Passover,
Cheering and laughing. We were all excited.
He hadn't changed that much. Some, but not that much.

    I guess you can't see what you think isn't there.

And it wasn't just him.

When you realize he's here even the food's different.
More important, I guess.
I don't know how to explain it.

You can't talk about things like that. There aren't words.
What you think's ordinary one minute is a miracle the next.
Nothing's changed. And everything has.

I cook meals every day, set them on the table.
That's my job, it's what everybody expects.
You just do it, you don't think about it.

But when I realized he was eating with us
It didn't seem so ordinary any more.
It was more than just food.

I can't explain it.
You'll have to come here and eat with us.
You're welcome any time.

But you have to change the way you look at things to see him.

And when you do
It's a whole new world.

Mary Magdalene

Mary is from Magdala, a fishing village on the Lake Galilee shore. Tradition says she had been a prostitute. She is now in her fifties, a woman who has regained her femininity in a strong, self-confident way— a woman who knows who she is. She is taller than average and carries herself with a regal bearing, although there is nothing of pride or a domineering spirit. She is dressed in a simple but elegant robe. Her voice combines great dignity and an immense calmness.

*THE BIBLICAL ACCOUNT
OF THE APPEARANCE TO MARY OF MAGDALA*

*On the first day of the week, Mary of Magdala came to the tomb
early in the morning, while it was still dark, and saw the stone removed
from the tomb. So she ran to Simon Peter and to the other disciple
whom Jesus loved, and told them, "They have taken the Lord from the
tomb, and we don't know where they put him. . . ."*

*They both ran. . . . Peter . . . went into the tomb and saw the burial
cloths there, and the cloth that had covered his head . . . rolled up in
a separate place. . . . Then the disciples returned home.*

*But Mary stayed outside the tomb weeping. And as she wept, she
bent over into the tomb and saw two angels in white sitting there, one
at the head and one at the feet where the body of Jesus had been.
And they said to her, "Woman, why are you weeping?"*

*She said to them, "They have taken my Lord, and I don't know
where they laid him." When she had said this, she turned around and
saw Jesus there, but did not know it was Jesus.*

*Jesus said to her, "Woman, why are you weeping? Whom are you
looking for?" She thought it was the gardener and she said to him, "Sir,
if you carried him away, tell me where you laid him and I will take him."*

*Jesus said to her, "Mary!" She turned and said to him in Hebrew,
"Rabbouni," which means Teacher. Jesus said to her, "Stop holding on
to me, for I have not yet ascended to the Father. But go to my brothers
and tell them. . . ."*

*Mary of Magdala went and announced to the disciples, "I have seen
the Lord," and what he told her.*

JOHN 20:1–18

The Biblical Account
of a Woman Caught in Adultery

Early in the morning he arrived again in the temple area, and all the people started coming to him, and he sat down and taught them. Then the scribes and the Pharisees brought a woman who had been caught in adultery and made her stand in the middle.

They said to him, "Teacher, this woman was caught in the very act of committing adultery. Now in the law, Moses commanded us to stone such women. So what do you say?"

They said this to test him, so that they could have some charge to bring against him.

Jesus bent down and began to write on the ground with his finger. But when they continued asking him, he straightened up and said to them, "Let the one among you who is without sin be the first to throw a stone at her."

Again he bent down and wrote on the ground. And in response, they went away one by one, beginning with the elders.

So he was left alone with the woman before him. Then Jesus straightened up and said to her, "Woman, where are they? Has no one condemned you?"

She replied, "No one, sir." Then Jesus said, "Neither do I condemn you. Go, [and] from now on, do not sin anymore."

MARY MAGDALENE

I loved him as the others did not,
    that is why I was at the tomb when they were not,
Standing at the door weeping when he came
    and he called my name, and I went to embrace him,
Happy as only those who have themselves been raised from the
    dead can be.

That is the last time we were together;
    he became a sacred memory then, served now by celibate men,
And I was made a saint, and stood upon a porcelain pedestal,
    divorced from him by those who live alone in arid deserts
As though he, like they, were above that love which most makes
    us human.

We did not think this, those of us who knew him,
    and he us, who traveled with him those hot and weary days.
At night we shared his rooms, and ate with him at one table,
    and I knew him then as a woman knows a man, and he me,
The knowledge of nakedness, without pretense or platitude.

And if there were words for sorrow I would tell you
    how my heart broke into
    a smashed and bleeding stone that day,
Watching the soldiers pound nails through his hands,
    watching the slow blood drip away, and the life going out
Of one who was for me all he is to you,

                And my lover as well.

I know the question you are asking. You need not ask it,
   for surely I no less than you am woman, and understand
How a woman must conquer in the dark world of mystery
   which we bear about within us, like a womb,
   the realm of the moon
Which waxes and wanes each month,
   and marks the calendar of the night.

In my village by the sea, I was hated for a witch, they said,
   or worse,
   but at night the men came to me while the women knitted,
Knowing as well as I how badly the man wants to
   be conquered,
   the emptiness in his soul because he is not woman.
Yet afraid (as I was too) to do what I did, they continued to knit.

Of course I tried to seduce him, and could have, had I chosen it,
   for he trusted himself to me, no less than to Judas.
And if I did not betray him, as Judas did, you may thank him,
   for it was he who took my power, did not do battle
As though to be a man consists of not being a woman,
   nor needing one.

Have you ever sat all night with a man's head in your lap
   (it is to my sisters that I speak), knowing his body is yours,
Knowing what a woman knows as she knows her own breasts,
   that within her body she carries the power of life and death,
That what is given cannot be taken,
   that a woman is more than a body

         And love is more than sex.

I did not understand that when first we met,
    and he looked into my eyes, and our souls were joined;
Love meant for me the ultimate intimacy, and I did not deny it;
    the moan of ecstasy has often risen from my hips
    into my throat,
I have known the joy of a man's body in mine, and his joy with me.

It is a profound and beautiful thing,
    the song which Solomon sang,
    but always there is the lacerating ripping apart,
The tissues once joined now parted,
    and the seed dying on my thighs
    for surely it is true,
    I have had many lovers and never been loved,
Each time feeling in some mysterious way
    a traitor to my own body.

I thought of him often as the father of my children,
    as you would have, for he loved them very much, and they him.
He listened to them as adults seldom do,
    and could have been their father
    had that been his destiny, as it was not,
For he belonged to all the world, as a father belongs to one woman.

Is that why you say, "He was not a man as I am,"
    that he did not create a family he could not care for?
Surely you too know that passion
    has very much to do
    with motherhood,
    that love has consequences which live, and if he could not stay
To finish what lovers in bed begin, he could not enter me,

He loved me too much.

I plead with you to listen! It is the same "good people,"
    those who once covered their faces when we met in the streets,
Who have made me one of them now;
    how I laugh to hear you call them "religious,"
    those who reduce life to a formula,
Those who have never lived yet know how others should live.

It was they who dragged into the temple a woman nearly naked,
    taken uncombed from her lover's bed
    like some loathsome beast;
"We have caught her in the very act!" they said,
    their faces betraying great pornographic glee.
(I do not think it was an accident their finding her there,
    and unclothed.)

They stood around her, an angry circle of rigid men
    armed with cruel stones, while she, already dead,
Defended her breasts and bowed her head,
    feeling the terror of passion denied,
    flowing from every pore like lightning unflashed
    in a desert storm.
I know, I was there.

Then he knelt to the ground and touched it with his finger,
    drawing on the earth the sign of two lines crossing
And we felt the anger slowly drain away,
    creating a space around us we did not know was there
Until the cathedral at Chartres was built, many centuries later.

That too was a labor of love.

part four

THE PALACE

alaces are where our societies are formed, where we make the choices that give our cultures shape and structure. Here change is most difficult and most strongly resisted, for whenever cultures change some people lose power and others gain power. It was in the palaces of his time that Jesus was sentenced to death, and it is here where we still find it hardest to make a place for him.

Zacchaeus
the Tax Collector

The tax collector's body is bent over with a congenital deformity, as if carrying on his shoulders all the dislike we have for government itself. He accepts the distaste others have for his work, but he also knows his contribution to human society is an essential one. Although disliked, he is not bitter and smiles often. He is serious; he knows the questions raised by his meeting with Jesus involve human survival itself. His voice is masculine and deliberate. His clothing indicates wealth, but not ostentation.

137

THE BIBLICAL ACCOUNT
OF ZACCHAEUS THE TAX COLLECTOR

He came to Jericho and intended to pass through the town. Now a man there named Zacchaeus, who was a chief tax collector and also a wealthy man, was seeking to see who Jesus was; but he could not see him because of the crowd, for he was short in stature.

So he ran ahead and climbed a sycamore tree in order to see Jesus, who was about to pass that way.

When he reached the place, Jesus looked up and said to him, "Zacchaeus, come down quickly, for today I must stay at your house." And he came down quickly and received him with joy.

When they all saw this, they began to grumble, saying, "He has gone to stay at the house of a sinner."

But Zacchaeus stood there and said to the Lord, "Behold, half of my possessions, Lord, I shall give to the poor, and if I have extorted anything from anyone I shall repay it four times over."

And Jesus said to him, "Today salvation has come to this house because this man too is a descendant of Abraham."

LUKE 19:1–9

Zacchaeus the Tax Collector

How much I resented it all.
Misshapen in my mother's womb,
Hated by my father for being short,
I hated myself for being hated.

My job was despised, and I despised myself for doing it.
And my neighbors for making me do it.

But somebody has to.
The soft-hearted and sentimental can't govern
And the cruel only destroy.

If I'm a tax collector it's because taxes have to be collected.
And if you hate me it's only because you hate your own state.

How quickly belonging to the public becomes a burden.
And how quickly we shrug it off onto hired hands,
Then hate the hands we have hired.

Do you complainers really think you can live on your dislikes?

Don't expect poetry from me, I work all day with unpaid bills.
And I'm not a lovable eccentric.
Such do not become rich farming the taxes.
 Indeed they usually have no taxes to pay.
 Even the Romans cannot tax poverty.

If I was wealthy there was a reason.
And I was quite wealthy.
But I was not happy.

Only my resentment made it possible to go on
Day after day, doing what had to be done.

When one sees life as impossibly awful
There is a perverse pleasure in enduring the pain,
And I had reached the point where I expected rejection.

When I heard he was coming I assumed he would ignore me.
I wanted to see him but expected it would come to nothing,
Only another disappointment.

I wasn't in the crowd that day.
Why stand there with people who hate you,
Especially when you can't see?

But there was an old tree I remembered from my boyhood,
The one I used to climb when the taunting grew too cruel.
There I can see, I thought, without being seen.

But when he came to my tree a strange thing happened.
Our eyes met and I saw there was no anger in them.
He wanted to be a guest at my house, he said.

I hardly knew how to act,
Suddenly to move from the outside, to be wanted.

It's hard to say who was more amazed, my neighbors or I.
We both had thought my situation hopeless.

   While he was eating at my house
   I asked him why he came to visit me.

   He told me we needed him.

Pilate's Wife

This is a bottom-line woman. Although she holds herself erect, she is not regal. Her place is to carry out orders, not give them, and she accepts her role as a given, attempting to make the best of it. Her clothing suggests wealth, but also a solid practicality. Her face is firm but relaxed, and her voice strong but not commanding. As she speaks she walks about her home, looking at its palatial furnishings with a certain detachment. She sees herself as a pawn, a player in a powerful game she understands but can only observe.

Jesus stood before [Pilate] the governor, and he questioned him, "Are you the king of the Jews?" Jesus said, "You say so." And when he was accused by the chief priests and elders, he made no answer.

Then Pilate said to him, "Do you not hear how many things they are testifying against you?" But he did not answer him one word, so that the governor was greatly amazed. . . .

While [Pilate] was still seated on the bench, his wife sent him a message, "Have nothing to do with that righteous man. I suffered much in a dream today because of him."

The chief priests and the elders persuaded the crowds to ask . . . to destroy Jesus. . . . They all said, "Let him be crucified!" But Pilate said, "Why? What evil has he done?" They only shouted the louder, "Let him be crucified!"

When Pilate saw that he was not succeeding at all, but that a riot was breaking out instead, he took water and washed his hands in the sight of the crowd, saying, "I am innocent of this man's blood. Look to it yourselves."

And the whole people said in reply, "His blood be upon us and upon our children."

Then . . . after he had Jesus scourged, he handed him over to be crucified.

Matthew 27:11–26

PILATE'S WIFE

We only did what had to be done.
Somebody had to do it.

We never wanted to get stuck out here in the first place.
It's hot and dirty, and dirt poor. The people hate us.
Even if they didn't they speak this weird language.

I wanted to go home, enjoy life while we still could.
But my husband said, "You wanna go back without any money?
You wanna live the way we used to?"

And he's right. Either you boss people around or they boss you.
So we tried to keep the lid on,
Go home with some money in our pocket.

But these people are impossible.
You never know what they'll do.

Everywhere else people live and let live,
Here they think there's only one way.
They won't do it our way and they can't decide what theirs is.

Then they want us to settle their arguments.
My husband is always talking about their crazy squabbles.
Every night there's some new one.

He rolls his eyes, rubs his head,
We try to figure out what to do.
If there's trouble we go back to Rome.
And then we're in trouble. Big trouble.

The only people think we've got power
Are the ones who keep asking us for favors.
Once you sit on these thrones you realize they're just fancy chairs
     Made by second-rate artists for the highest bidder.

All week we'd been trying to figure out what to do with this Jesus.
If we put him in jail there'd be a riot,
If we didn't nobody knew what would happen.

The priests kept coming in saying, "You've got to do something."
Why they thought he was dangerous we couldn't see,
He didn't have a single soldier.

Once I sent a servant girl, one that spoke his language.
I said, "Find out what he's saying." What she said was
The only way to change the world is for us to change.

That night I had a terrible nightmare.
It woke me up so I couldn't sleep anymore.
Then I heard the priests brought him in, wanted us to kill him.

I knew it wouldn't work.
My servant girl was too excited telling me what she'd heard.
You can't kill that.

But if he hadn't died we would have.
And what good would that have done anybody?
They'd just send somebody else,
There's always somebody wants to live in the palace.

               They think there's power here.
               But what you find out is
               It's just an empty chair.

The High Priest's Sister

The high priest's sister is an older woman, wearing expensive heirloom jewelry passed down in her family for many generations. Had she been a European she would have belonged to an aristocratic family, related to royalty. Had she lived in the United States she would have belonged to one of the old money families. She believes her overriding responsibility is to her social class, and that its responsibility is to ensure political and social continuity. She speaks with both strength and resignation.

THE BIBLICAL ACCOUNT
OF THE SESSION OF THE SANHEDRIN

Now many of the Jews who had come to Mary and seen what he had done began to believe in him. But some of them went to the Pharisees and told them what Jesus had done.

So the chief priests and the Pharisees convened the Sanhedrin and said, "What are we going to do? This man is performing many signs. If we leave him alone, all will believe in him, and the Romans will come and take away both our land and our nation."

But one of them, Caiaphas, who was high priest that year, said to them, "You know nothing, nor do you consider that it is better for you that one man should die instead of the people, so that the whole nation may not perish."

So from that day on they planned to kill him.

JOHN 11:45–50, 53

THE HIGH PRIEST'S SISTER

We didn't want to kill him, but we had no choice.
Nobody understood how precarious our position was.
They thought their hair-splitting debates were all that mattered.

But we had the temple to worry about.
Built at such great cost, it was all we had left.
What would you have thought had we risked this great building
Just to save some backwoods preacher?

He wasn't the first one. Every few years they came to town
Making promises they couldn't keep.
They left as quickly as they came
And we'd have to deal with the chaos they left behind.

   They thought it their business to criticize us,
   But had we not preserved order
   How could they have preached?

Of course there were ample grounds for complaint,
We knew that better than they. The income from our estates
Had fallen off precipitously since the Romans came.

But when we resisted
They just sent more soldiers and it was only worse.
It's irresponsible to upset people like that,
Starting these silly little revolts as though survival doesn't matter.

We existed because the Romans permitted us to exist,
And the temple was open only because we cooperated
With the military.

         There was no other way.

Would you have let him dismantle society,
Then try to rebuild it some new way
With no proof of his credentials?

We haven't survived all these centuries
Taking rash and dangerous risks like that.
The temple was entrusted to us
And we intended to pass it on intact and unchanged.

    Once before it had been destroyed
    When our forebears disobeyed the laws
    And we did not intend to repeat their terrible error.

Of course we would have preferred being spared
This unpleasant duty.
Indeed, we had tried repeatedly to urge him to moderation.
There was no reason he couldn't continue his good works
    among the sick.

But he would not compromise.
He seemed to believe there was some new way to order the world.
Exactly what it was we did not know,
Much less whether it would work.

And so we had to remove him from the scene.

Had we not done so we ourselves would have been killed.
And what good would that have done anyone?

        Agreed, it was a messy and disreputable affair.
        But what other choice did we have?
        Except give up our authority
        And follow him ourselves.

The Carpenter's Daughter

The carpenter's daughter is a young woman, bony and muscular but not unattractive. She works with her hands, and understands that persons who do so are essential to society. She takes a quiet pride in her family's contribution, but has also learned from an early age that "the customer is always right." As she speaks she moves about the room picking up things, looking at how they are made, setting them down carefully. Her clothing is simple but substantial, indicating a person who is neither rich nor poor. Her voice is matter of fact.

THE BIBLICAL ACCOUNT
OF THE WAY OF THE CROSS

So [Pilate] released the man who had been imprisoned for rebellion and murder, for whom they asked, and he handed Jesus over to them to deal with as they wished.

As they led him away they took hold of a certain Simon, a Cyrenian, who was coming in from the country; and after laying the cross on him, they made him carry it behind Jesus.

A large crowd of people followed Jesus, including many women who mourned and lamented him. Jesus turned to them and said, "Daughters of Jerusalem, do not weep for me; weep instead for yourselves and for your children. . . ."

When they came to the place called the Skull, they crucified him and the criminals there, one on his right, the other on his left. . . . The people stood by and watched; the rulers, meanwhile, sneered at him and said, "He saved others, let him save himself if he is the chosen one, the Messiah of God." Even the soldiers jeered at him. As they approached to offer him wine they called out, "If you are King of the Jews, save yourself."

Above him there was an inscription that read, "This is the King of the Jews."

Luke 23:25–38

THE CARPENTER'S DAUGHTER

We make our living making things.
Sure, we'd rather make baby cribs and ox yokes,
But that's not what they want. We gotta pay for our food too.

And they don't ask if you wanna, they just tell you.
The Romans like their crosses big and heavy;
The colonel told my dad they're supposed to scare people.

You have to find a big tree and then cut it just right.
The whole family worked on it all week.
We was all sorta proud when we got done.

Then the soldiers came and paid us.
We got all busy makin' other stuff, you know,
And we didn't think about it any more.

Until that mornin' I was cleanin' up for Passover.
There was a lotta noise outside, and this crowd—
All kinds a people headin' toward the cemetery.
Some was soldiers but mostly people just watchin'.

And in the middle was this guy carryin' a cross.
They half kill you with a whip,
Then they make you carry your own cross.
People stand around makin' fun—they do it all the time.

    But then I saw it was our cross.
    You could tell the way we cut the wood,
    The way we fastened it together.

And the guy carryin' it, I kinda recognized him too.
He was all bloody, layin' on the ground.

But you could tell he's the rabbi everybody's talkin' about.
Some say he's the one we're waitin' for to be free.
Everybody says he helps people, when he talks it makes sense.

And now here he is with the soldiers beatin' on him,
And our people makin' fun a him.

You could see he couldn't go on.
But then the soldiers grab this black guy,
Make him carry it instead.

Since it was our cross I decided to follow along,
See what happened.

They take off all your clothes, pound nails through your hands.
You hang there naked, dyin', with a rope around your chest.
Only low class people, like slaves, they do that to.
Or dangerous people, like startin' a revolution.

His mother was there watchin'. That's what got me.
I wanted to tell her I was sorry, us makin' the cross and all.
But what was I supposed to say?

If we hadn't a made it they'd a killed us.
And what good would that a done anybody?

   When I got home everybody asked me where I was.
   I didn't want a tell 'em. But I had to.

      I said I was watchin' Jesus die on our cross.

Barabbas

Barabbas is muscular and charismatic, a true warrior. Like an athlete, he is accustomed to the crowd's adulation. He is dressed in combat fatigues and is armed. He does not want to kill, but is able to do so when necessary. His speech is slow and deliberate, marked by the quiet dignity that comes from having one's courage tested in battle on numerous occasions. As he speaks he glances over his shoulder at the door, as though to guard it.

THE BIBLICAL ACCOUNT
OF THE RELEASE OF BARABBAS

On the occasion of the feast the governor was accustomed to release to the crowd one prisoner whom they wished. And at that time they had a notorious prisoner called [Jesus] Barabbas.

So when they had assembled, Pilate said to them, "Which one do you want me to release to you, [Jesus] Barabbas, or Jesus called Messiah?" . . . They answered, "Barabbas!"

Pilate said to them, "Then what shall I do with Jesus called Messiah?" They all said, "Let him be crucified!"

But he said, "Why? What evil has he done?" They only shouted the louder, "Let him be crucified!"

When Pilate saw that he was not succeeding at all, but that a riot was breaking out instead, he took water and washed his hands in the sight of the crowd, saying, "I am innocent of this man's blood. . . ."

Then he released Barabbas to them, but after he had Jesus scourged, he handed him over to be crucified.

MATTHEW 27:15–26

BARABBAS

My name is Barabbas.
He died instead of me.
It wasn't fair. And I felt bad.
But then I was willing to die for him.
That's what bein' a soldier's all about.

Nothin' ever changes unless somebody's ready to die.
The bullies run everything otherwise.
It's always been that way, it'll always be that way.
You hate seein' people get killed, but there's no choice.
Except let the bad guys run the world.

What I couldn't understand was
Why didn't he fight back?
An eye for an eye, a tooth for a tooth,
That's the only thing they understand.
Try to be nice and they'll spit in your face, rob you blind.

We heard a him but didn't pay much attention.
Too busy fightin' the Romans to listen to sermons.
It's nice to be lovey-dovey and all that,
But somebody's gotta win the war.

I figured him a coward.
But watchin' a man die you see what he's made of.
The cowards whine and slobber, go limp when it's time.
A real soldier knows that's what he's here for—
To die so others don't have to.

Even up there on the cross, hurtin' real bad,
He was thinkin' about other people.

It takes more than tough to do that.
I was watchin' the Roman officer;
You could see him thinkin' the same thing.

They didn't kill him.
He was the one decided to die.
Who has that kind a power?
The Roman finally said, "He must be some kinda god."
We all thought the same.

I went on fightin' after that, but it didn't make sense.
Every time I'd waste somebody I'd think about him,
Realize how weak we really was.
I kill you, you kill me. Does this really change anything?
Who's gonna win all these wars?

It's for sure he had a different way,
But I never could figure it out what it was.
I talked to a preacher once, he told me how to die.
But I already knew that.
What I want a know is how we're supposed to win.

   He knew that and I don't.

The
Servant Girl

The servant girl is tough and cynical. She believes life is predetermined, that some people are born lucky and others unlucky, and the most the unlucky can hope for is to be abused as little as possible. Her philosophy is "things happen and we react." She is short and wears workingwoman's clothing, carrying herself with confidence, and even a certain authority. Her voice is strong, although it often conveys resignation and a deep anger. She accepts things as they are but has little respect for the way the world's affairs are conducted.

The Biblical Account
of Peter's Denial of Jesus

After arresting him they led him away and took him into the house of the high priest; Peter was following at a distance.

They lit a fire in the middle of the courtyard and sat around it, and Peter sat down with them.

When a maid saw him seated in the light, she looked intently at him and said, "This man too was with him." But he denied it saying, "Woman, I do not know him."

A short while later someone else saw him and said, "You too are one of them"; but Peter answered, "My friend, I am not."

About an hour later, still another insisted, "Assuredly, this man too was with him, for he also is a Galilean." But Peter said, "My friend, I do not know what you are talking about."

Just as he was saying this, the cock crowed, and the Lord turned and looked at Peter; and Peter remembered the word of the Lord, how he had said to him, "Before the cock crows today, you will deny me three times."

He went out and began to weep bitterly.

Luke 22:54–62

THE SERVANT GIRL

It was quite a night.
The whole town was like to blow up any minute.
They was afraid to arrest him and afraid not to.
Our guys went out scared to death,
Coulda started a riot or somethin', got themselves killed.

We couldn't a done a thing except one a his guys sold him out.
Sure it was dirty, but you can't blame him.
You gotta do what you gotta do. It's all fate.
There's some supposed to be rich and some not.
If you ain't lucky you take what you can get.

My family and us we worked for the high priest.
We didn't have nothin' and they was always tryin' to take that.
But sometimes they'd give us their old clothes,
Or some old food they didn't want.
It wasn't bad.

I was supposed to watch the door while he was up with the suits
But this guy I knew kinda sweet-talked his way in. And his buddy.
I shouldn't a let 'em in but I felt sorry for 'em,
Thinkin' this was their lucky break and everything.
Then standin' out in the cold like that.

This guy's made outta brass. Sits down right by the fire.
Then my sister tells me he's the one they call Rocky.
Practically cut off cousin Malchus's ear.
Well, now I'm mad. So I looks him right in the face,
I says, "You're one a his men. Ain't you?"

But he acts like he don't know what I'm talkin' about.
We was all rollin' our eyes. Even the way he talked
You could tell he belonged to them.

About dawn they brought Jesus down to where we was.
The guys had beat him up pretty good.
Some was makin' fun. Slappin' him around and like that.
But every time they hit him he just looked sadder.
It really got to you after awhile.

This Rocky guy just sits there by the fire the whole time.
I guess he's thinkin', "Nothin' I can do, may as well keep warm."
We keep tellin' him, "We know you came here with him.
Admit it." But he keeps actin' like he's one a us.

Then the rooster starts crowin' and he sees Jesus lookin' at him.
You shoulda seen the look on that Rocky's face.
Jumps up, yanks the door open like he's gettin' out a jail,
Start's bawlin' his eyes out, runnin' down the street.

So now I start lookin' at Jesus myself,
And I see him lookin' at me.
It gets to you. And it don't go away.
The older you get the more you think about it.

   I tell you honestly
   What I want a know now is
   Whatever happened to that Rocky guy?

      Why was he cryin'?
      And where was he goin'?
      And did he ever quit bein' such a phony?

The
Sergeant

The sergeant is weathered and tough,
accustomed to battle and to difficult
situations. He is at midlife, athletic, sandy-
haired, and speaks with a drawl. He is a
man who has moved from a life of poverty
at the edges of empire to a position of
modest power by accepting orders from his
superiors. His voice and movements
convey a real self-confidence, which is
based on his success in finding effective
ways to carry out the orders he receives.
He is dressed in a military uniform with
a rifle across his shoulder.

The Biblical Account
of the Burial and Resurrection of Jesus

When it was evening, there came a rich man from Arimathea named Joseph, who was himself a disciple of Jesus. He went to Pilate and asked for the body of Jesus. ... Joseph wrapped it [in] clean linen and laid it in his new tomb that he had hewn in the rock. Then he rolled a huge stone across the entrance to the tomb and departed. ...

The next day, the chief priests and the Pharisees gathered before Pilate and said, "Sir, we remember that this imposter while still alive said, 'After three days I will be raised up.' Give orders, then, that the grave be secured until the third day, lest his disciples come and steal him and say to the people, 'He has been raised from the dead. ...'"

Pilate said to them, "The guard is yours; go secure it as best you can." So they went and secured the tomb by fixing a seal to the stone and setting the guard. ...

And behold, there was a great earthquake; for an angel of the Lord descended from heaven, approached, rolled back the stone, and sat upon it. His appearance was like lightning and his clothing was white as snow. The guards were shaken with fear of him and became like dead men. ...

Some of the guard went into the city and told the chief priests all that had happened. They assembled with the elders and took counsel; then they gave a large sum of money to the soldiers, telling them, "You are to say, 'His disciples came by night and stole him while we were asleep.' And if this gets to the ears of the governor, we will satisfy [him] and keep you out of trouble."

The soldiers took the money and did as they were instructed.

Matthew 27:57–28:15

THE SERGEANT

That tomb was empty.
And what was I supposed to tell the captain?
He don't take kindly to excuses.

That somebody was dead all a sudden got up,
Pushed a tomb open and walked out?
And we couldn't do nothin' about it?

When we come to we was so piss-in-our-britches scared
We just plumb run away. It weren't pretty.
And what was I supposed to tell my men? Nothin' happened?

Ole Festus was like to wake the dead howlin' out loud.
Threw his sword in the bushes, put his hands top a his head,
Headed for the hills.

Fact is, we was all sleepin'.
Had some a 'em leanin' on the tomb.
Figured if anybody tried gettin' in they'd wake us up.

Who ever heard a anything happenin' *inside* a tomb?

What woke us up was the light.
The ground starts shakin', we all start fallin' down,
Puttin' our arms over our faces. Thought we was goners for sure.

When it was over I told 'em to light a torch.
Sure enough, that tomb was as empty as they get.
The cloth they wrapped him up in was layin' on the bench.

Sometimes you hear people gettin' buried ain't dead.
But that stone took six, seven men with sticks to move.
And I put a spear in his guts myself.
If he was still alive he was too sick to move.

Hey, this is the army. We don't take chances.
People hear a story like that, they're like to go crazy.
Might start a revolution or somethin'.

But we had a say somethin'.
I ain't proud a what we did, but we didn't have no choice.
They called us in, gave us a lot a money, told us what to say.

    But when you seen something you seen it.
    Lies don't change facts.
    Neither does closin' your eyes.

    But what was we supposed to do?
    If we'd a told the truth they'd a killed us.
    And what good would that a done anybody?

We went on like before. Takin' orders.
Gettin' drunk on payday. Hopin' we'd get home before we died.
Grunts don't expect much.

Except for ole Festus. Never did see him again.
Went lookin' all over for him. Never found hide nor hair.
Some said they saw him with the ones said it was true.

        Others said they saw him gettin' on a boat.
        Told 'em he was goin' back home
        To Ireland.

Judas
Iscariot

Judas is energetic and intelligent, a man who knows how to get things done. He is also practical, able to quickly distinguish fantasy from reality—the opposite of a dreamer. He is dressed as a business executive, but his actions do not suggest a commanding attitude. He has been profoundly humbled by his experience, and comes to tell us what he has learned. He is guilty and knows it, but also knows he has an urgent message to convey. He often looks down at the floor as he speaks. His voice is deep and strong, but gentle.

THE BIBLICAL ACCOUNT
OF THE BETRAYAL AND ARREST OF JESUS

Then one of the Twelve, who was called Judas Iscariot, went to the chief priests and said, "What are you willing to give me if I hand him over to you?" They paid him thirty pieces of silver, and from that time on he looked for an opportunity to hand him over.

On the first day of the Feast of Unleavened Bread, . . . he reclined at table with the Twelve. And while they were eating, he said, "Amen, I say to you, one of you will betray me." Deeply distressed at this, they began to say to him one after another, "Surely it is not I, Lord?" He said in reply, "He who has dipped his hand into the dish with me is the one who will betray me. . . ."

Then Judas, his betrayer, said in reply, "Surely it is not I, Rabbi?" He answered, "You have said so."

* * * *

While he was still speaking, Judas, one of the Twelve, arrived, accompanied by a large crowd, with swords and clubs. . . . Immediately he went over to Jesus and said, "Hail, Rabbi!" and he kissed him.

Jesus answered him, "Friend, do what you have come for." Then stepping forward they laid hands on Jesus and arrested him.

And behold, one of those who accompanied Jesus put his hand to his sword, drew it, and struck the high priest's servant, cutting off his ear. Then Jesus said, "Put your sword back into its sheath, for all who take the sword will perish by the sword. . . ."

Then all the disciples left him and fled.

MATTHEW 26:14–25; 47–56

JUDAS ISCARIOT

Crazy as it sounds,
I thought I knew exactly what to do.

That with a few well-chosen elegant tricks,
And a lie told now and then,
I could manage anything.

[He shakes his head in disbelief.]

I know you think me merely a greedy traitor,
And so I was.
But the truth is even worse.

For I thought I understood power and he did not,
That his words were merely dreams meant to comfort us,
Not laws which could ever govern us.

"It's mean and nasty out there," I kept telling him,
"You've got to protect yourself.
People will rip you off, use you up, throw you away,
Leave you broke and abandoned."

"Be strong!" I told him, "don't be so loving!"

But what did I know about strength,
Never having had any?

Thinking power was merely the weak
Dominating the even weaker.

That is why I thought myself qualified to trick him.

Oh it was a grand scheme,
Worthy of Machiavelli himself.
I would bring the soldiers to him, force him to fight,

Face him with reality,
Make him forget the lofty ideals,
Turn him into a warrior.

Surely we would win.
With his power how could we lose?

And at first it worked.

I got there, walked up to him,
Kissed him on the cheek. He wasn't afraid.
Peter right away pulled out his sword, started hacking away.

Their soldiers didn't even try to fight.
It was a ragtag bunch. Didn't want to be there.
It wasn't their fight.

Peter left one guy's ear hanging off his head
Covered with blood, howling like a whipped dog.
The others threw up their arms, tried to hide.

I almost laughed out loud, it was so easy.
"We're headed for the top," I thought.
Once you start fighting there's no place to stop.

All it took was one word from him
And the revolution begins.

Then the soldier's torches lit his eyes and it was all over.
"People who kill get killed," he said to Peter.
"Put away your sword."

Then he turned to the man we had wounded,
Healing him.
Getting blood all over his hands.

We just stood there.
Nobody knew what to do.
We'd never seen anything like it.

Finally one of the officers started barking orders,
Scared to death.
Then they grabbed him and tied his hands.

Peter and the others ran off and it was just me.
    What could I do? I couldn't go with the soldiers,
    And I couldn't follow him anymore.

The money hung on my belt like a sack of blood.
I planned to buy weapons with it. But standing there
Alone in the Garden I realized weapons didn't matter
    anymore.

Desperation kept me going for a while.
I disguised myself and joined the mob at the palace.
    "Crucify him! Crucify him!" we shouted.
    "He tricked us, he let us down."

            Maybe the Romans could save him, I thought.
            And the governor tried. But what could he do?
            We insisted.

It was there at the palace, when Jesus looked at me,
I knew we had to make a change.

I left the crowd immediately,
Took the money back to the temple,
Threw it on the floor like garbage.

Then I hung myself.
It was the only thing I knew how to do.

What a fool.

We had to kill him,
It was the only way we could understand.
But I didn't have to commit suicide.
Even I could have been forgiven if I'd waited.

That was my great crime—
I refused the gift before I knew what it was.

And it wasn't just me.
We all betrayed him,
As he knew we would.

The others wanted power too, but without cost.
They kept giving him their lives,
And he kept giving them back to them to live.

But who else could he have chosen?
Nobody understood him. How could we have?
Who would we have learned it from?

We knew only the old ways
And could not imagine any other.

You hate me now.
And rightly so.

But there is much I can teach you.
I too am among the apostles,
Though not among the saints.

"Christ killer!" you call me,
And my people.
But are you really so different?

My guilt cannot be made less by showing you yours,
But neither can you excuse yours by hating me.

Don't you too spend money that belongs to the poor?
Don't you too dream and scheme rather than pray?
Don't you too say, "I'll follow you,"
        then try to change him?
Don't you too believe we know better than he how to live?

I had thought us totally alone,
Abandoned, with no one but ourselves to rely on.
That is why I did what I did.

But I could not have been more mistaken.

He is here.
Even when we have killed him, he is here.
And rises each day from the places we have buried him

        To give us a second chance.

The choice is yours now.

> You can follow him
> Or you can follow me.
>
> You can remain in charge
> And kill until the world is a barren waste.
>
> Or you can love,
> Creating life until the earth is a paradise.

It's got to end somehow.